D0537587

The Mountain Biker's Cookbook

Compiled and Written by Jill Smith-Gould

Library of Congress Cataloging-in-Publication Data

Smith-Gould, Jill 1970-
    The mountain biker's cookbook / compiled and written by Jill Smith-Gould.
        p.   cm.
    Includes index.
    ISBN 1-884737-22-6
    1. Cookery. 2. Low-fat diet—Recipes. 3. Cyclists. I. Title.
TX714.S597   1997
641.5'638–dc21

Printed in the U.S.A.

VeloPress
1830 N. 55th Street • Boulder, Colorado 80301-2700 • USA
303/440-0601 • FAX 303/444-6788 • e-mail: velonews@aol.com

To purchase additional copies of this book or other Velo products,
call 800/234-8356 (International call 303/440-0601, ext. 6).

Dedicated to bike racers everywhere

Thank-You

Nutrition contributors
Kelly Anne Carter-Erdman
Wilf Paish
Louis Passfield

Book design and illustrations
Rick Smith

Cover Design
Erin Johnson

Cover Photography
The Photo Works, Inc.

... and special thanks to Laurie Brandt for modeling

Thanks

I would like to have some ingenious way to sufficiently thank the many people whose contributions made this book possible. I'll just have to hope they all realize how much I appreciate their valuable assistance! Many, many thanks to the following World Cup competitors, family, and friends who enabled this project to happen.

Recipe contributors

Caroline Alexander • Sara Ballantyne • Laurie Brandt • Elladee Brown • Kelly Anne Carter Erdman • Nick and Sarah Craig • Penny Davidson • Susan DeMattei • Ernst and Claudia Denifl • Karen Dreaves • Gary Foord • Vera Gillis • Cynthia Gould • Tim Gould • Kim Hallum • Jonathon Holmes • Bill Hurley • Marc Kazimirski • Dr. Judy Kazimirski • Mike and Emily Kloser • Christian Lemmerz • Ruthie Matthes • Kate McLarty • Deb Murrell • Jacquie Phelan • Chrissy Redden • Shirley Richards • Sian Roberts • Nancy Smith • Marjorie Soares • Peter Stace-Smith • Alex Stieda • Martin Stenger • Alison Sydor • Margaret Violet • Angela Ward

Photo contributors

• Robert Oliver - Inside Communications • Jill Smith-Gould and Rick Smith - Quick & Dirty

Contents

This book
belongs to:

— — — — — — — —

About the Author

Jill, being a bit of a "Jack of all trades," got into sport early in life. She started skating and playing ice-hockey as a preschooler, which remains her favorite sport to this day. While in nursing school, from the ages of 16 to 19, she earned her green belt in Judo, then gave up sport altogether. After using a bike to commute to work, touring, and watching some road races, she launched a career in bike racing that has lasted 9 years. She has been on the Canadian National team, in either road or mountain bike, since 1989, and has travelled extensively to international competitions. Despite the arduous race schedule, she has continued to work as a nurse throughout her race career, holding the same job for the past 11 years. She has also found time to pursue her favorite hobbies (ice-hockey, running, hiking) and part-time university studies (history of philosophy, nutrition).

Always an avid eater, Jill relishes the Epicurean lifestyle of a bike racer. Cooking and baking are among her favorite past times, so she takes pleasure in cooking while travelling extensively to bike races. She especially likes cooking for teams of hungry mountain bikers, where she is most appreciated!

A note on the athlete-contributors

Throughout the book you will find short profiles on the 25 athlete contributors. The camaraderie and mutual respect within the mountain bike community made it relatively easy to approach other competitors about donating a recipe. This laid-back attitude reflects a healthy balance between professionalism and a realistic, relaxed approach that is so common with so many top mountain bike racers. The ability to put things in perspective is what ultimately allows for the best performance. Diet and training alone don't produce top athletes, but are part of a lifestyle that brings us closer to reaching our full potential. A big part of that equation is attitude, and once again I'd like to thank my fellow competitors for having such good ones!

Epicureans at heart, cyclists love food — and lots of it!

The best way to get reliable nutritious meals is to make them yourself.

In my experience, I've observed that most male riders learn two important skills when they begin racing: shaving their legs and cooking!

When people ask me how I came up with the idea of a cookbook for mountain bikers, the reply is always a bit vague and convoluted, but really it started because I was fed up with all the compliments about my cooking. Admittedly, I love to cook, and whether at home or on the road, I have always made a point to do my own cooking. However, it gets a bit embarrassing after a while, with people saying, "You should write a cookbook!" After several years of feeding bike racers and listening to these comments, I figured it was time to remedy the situation.

Following the decision to educate the masses in the area of food preparation, I decided to call in reinforcements. The response to my call for recipes was even better than I had hoped, and although this project started off as a cookbook for people who are afraid to cook, it soon expanded to involve all levels of culinary ability. On top of that, my old buddy, teammate and registered dietician, Kelly Anne Carter-Erdman was there to help out with the nutrition section, lending some weight to my rantings on eating a healthy diet. For the most part, the following recipes are low-fat and nutritious, but somehow, quite a number of decadent desserts managed to sneak their way into the sweets section.

The icing on the cake was provided by my "little" brother, Rick Smith. His original design and artwork were invaluable and gave my potentially boring old cookbook a bold new face. He even let me help with some of the drawings (whether I will ever forgive him for our self-published version of this book is another story...)!

So, to all you gourmet chefs in training and wanna-be world cup racers...get your asses in gear...train hard, race harder; cook well, eat better.

1

photo by Robert Oliver

Glossary

The first part of this chapter deals with kitchen basics such as supplies, cooking terms, and spices found throughout the cookbook. If you are already a "master chef", then skip this section and get cooking instead!

After you've tested a recipe once or twice, try out some different ingredients.

How to use recipes

When using a recipe for the first time:

(1) Read it through, noting the ingredients and approximately how long it will take to prepare.
(2) Gather the ingredients as indicated. If there are items you don't have, see if you can substitute them with something you have on hand.
(3) Prepare the recipe, and note any changes you might want to try for next time.

Most recipes in this book can be made with a small base of equipment.

Supplies

Some kitchen tools and appliances, such as a food processor, are mere luxuries to make preparation quicker. When cooking away from home, you are often without these little extras, so most of the recipes in this book use good old fashioned "manual" preparation methods.

No food processors were used (or abused) in the production of this book.

Always wash vegetables before further preparation.

Carrots can be lightly peeled by scraping the surface with a knife to get rid of any dirt.

If vegetables are the main course or focus of the dish, large pieces are best. If they are to be part of a sauce or casserole, the pieces should be smaller and cut to a uniform size.

Common abbreviations:

Tbsp. = tablespoon
tsp. = teaspoon
C. = cup
oz. = ounce
Fl. oz. = fluid ounce
qt. = quart
med. = medium
mod. = moderate
sl. = slightly
sm. = small
amt. = amount
mins. = minutes
opt. = optional
pkg. = package
b.soda = baking soda
b.powder = baking powder

Ingredient Preparation

• **Chopped** Ingredients should be chopped to consistent sizes, which vary depending on how they are being used. Smaller pieces will speed cooking time, while larger pieces stay crisp when cooked together.

• **Crushed** This usually refers to garlic, though some recipes require crushed spices or ginger. I prefer to finely chop, or grate garlic so it stays in distinct pieces and has more flavor when cooked. However, you may want to crush the garlic when using it raw, as in pesto sauce.

• **Diced** Cut into cubed pieces of consistent size.

• **Ground** Grinding usually refers to dried ingredients. You can use a good blender, pound ingredients with a rolling pin, or use a mortar and pestle.

• **Minced** Cut finely into very small pieces.

• **Sliced** Slice to medium thickness, unless otherwise stated. To slice finely use a thin, sharp knife, or a grater with a straight slotted side.

Liquid Measure Guide

U.S. cups are slightly less than Imperial cups (235 ml instead of 250ml). Most of the recipes in this book use Imperial; However, the difference is only 6%, which becomes insignificant with volumes less than half a cup.

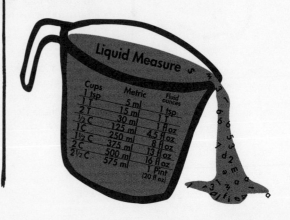

Cups	Metric	Fluid ounces
1 tsp	5 ml	1 tsp
1 T	15 ml	1 T
2 T	30 ml	1 fl oz
½ C	125 ml	4.5 fl oz
1 C	250 ml	8 fl oz
1½ C	375 ml	13 fl oz
2 C	500 ml	16 fl oz
2½ C	575 ml	1 Pint (20 fl oz)

"Roosting" Techniques

Bake: To blow up in a race. Also known as being cooked, fried or toasted.

Beat: To punish your opponents by starting fast and staying in front for the duration of a race.

Roast: To race very fast (and win)!

Season: The months when there are serious races to attend (usually between April and October).

Tender-crisp: Similar to "Big Al" Dente.

I've "translated" the temperatures found in the recipes into Fahrenheit for North American chefs. This little oven guide is mostly for the "Euros" who use celsius, and the "Brits" with their mysterious system of gas marks.

Cooking Techniques

- **Al dente** To cook pasta so it is still firm when bitten into. Literally means "to the tooth."

- **Bake** To cook in an oven.

- **Beat** To stir well, creating a creamy consistency.

- **Boil** To cook in an ample amount of boiling water. Used for rice, pasta, and some vegetables.

- **Par-boil** To briefly cook in boiling water, before roasting, baking, or freezing.

- **Purée** To mash or blend food to a uniform mass.

- **Roast** To cook raw food in the oven without the addition of liquid.

- **Sauté** To fry rapidly in hot, shallow oil while moving or tossing the food to heat it evenly.

- **Season "to taste"** This means to add seasonings such as salt and pepper in amounts that you prefer. Foods need to be "taste tested" due to variations in ingredients and individual preferences.

- **Stir-fry** To cook rapidly in hot oil without browning, preserving the taste, texture and nutrients.

- **Tender-crisp** To cook vegetables until almost tender, but still a little crispy.

Oven Temperature Guide

F°	C°	Gas mark
200	95	1/4
250	120	1/2
300	150	2 (cool)
350	175	4
400	205	6
450	230	8 (hot)
475	245	9 (hotter)

If gas marks aren't bad enough, now this "obscure" British way of measuring ingredients!

When I first moved to Britain, I couldn't believe people actually had scales and weighed all their ingredients. "What a waste of time" I thought to myself.

By the time I had baked a few biscuits and made my first sticky toffee pudding, I had to reconsider! Surprisingly, it really is easier, and more accurate to bake using kitchen scales. Instead of having to squish soft butter into appropriate-sized measuring cups, you just place it on the scale!

To make things easier, I've translated all the recipes into North American equivalents.

However, since there are so many British-contributed recipes, I have left the Imperial measures in with those recipes for quick reference.

Dry Measures Guide

I tried to make this more exciting, but it's still just another dry measures guide! (An approximate volume and weight-measurement chart for ingredients used in this cookbook.) Keep in mind that these are approximate equivalent measures only! The weights really are accurate, so sometimes it's difficult to find the exact cup fraction to match.

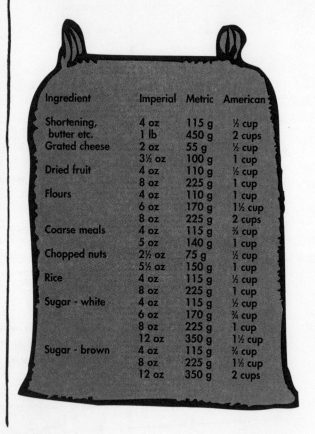

Ingredient	Imperial	Metric	American
Shortening, butter etc.	4 oz	115 g	½ cup
	1 lb	450 g	2 cups
Grated cheese	2 oz	55 g	½ cup
	3½ oz	100 g	1 cup
Dried fruit	4 oz	110 g	½ cup
	8 oz	225 g	1 cup
Flours	4 oz	110 g	1 cup
	6 oz	170 g	1½ cup
	8 oz	225 g	2 cups
Coarse meals	4 oz	115 g	¾ cup
	5 oz	140 g	1 cup
Chopped nuts	2½ oz	75 g	½ cup
	5½ oz	150 g	1 cup
Rice	4 oz	115 g	½ cup
	8 oz	225 g	1 cup
Sugar - white	4 oz	115 g	½ cup
	6 oz	170 g	¾ cup
	8 oz	225 g	1 cup
	12 oz	350 g	1½ cup
Sugar - brown	4 oz	115 g	¾ cup
	8 oz	225 g	1½ cup
	12 oz	350 g	2 cups

Ingredient Guide

This describes some of the ingredients found in the following recipes

- **Cous-cous** A wheat product similar in texture to rice, cous-cous is very quick to cook. It can be used in both sweet and savory dishes.

- **Miso** Made from fermented soy beans, miso is distinctively flavored, quick to prepare, and nourishing. It can also be made from other fermented grains, such as rice or wheat. Soy miso is available in dark, medium or light. It is usually used as a soup base, but can also be used for flavoring, as in miso gravy, or with rice.

- **Tahini** A peanut butter-like spread made from sesame seeds. It is available light (unroasted) or dark (roasted). Both are used in these recipes.

- **Tofu** Tofu (or bean curd) is light tasting, acquires flavors readily, and has a wide range of uses. It is high in protein, low in fat, easy to digest, quick to cook and versatile. Available soft or firm, packaged, bulk, smoked, herbed, deep fried or as a prepared food such as tofu-burgers or hot dogs.

- **Vegetable oil** This is a generic term to describe the many oils that are made from crops such as sunflower or rape seed (Canola) oil. They are good for shallow or deep frying.

- **Peanut oil** Peanut oil is best for stir-frying since it can be heated to a very high temperature.

- **Olive oil** "Virgin" is best used unheated, since it loses its distinct taste once cooked. Light or regular olive oil can be used for lightly fried foods and is great for sautéing garlic and onions.

- **Sesame oil** A very pungent oil, so only a little is needed. Used to add flavor to stir-fries or tofu.

Miso is the perfect "fast food". It provides sustenance, yet is quick and simple to prepare. Find it in health food stores, oriental shops and some deli's.

You can try reducing the amount of oil suggested in given recipes unless there is a noticeable flavor loss.

Top tip: Try using applesauce or mashed banana in place of oil when baking.

7

Herbs and Spices

This describes some of some of the herbs and spices used in the following recipes.

Sample uses:

Pasta sauces
Pesto sauce
Caprese salad

- **Basil** This distinctive herb is used in a variety of savory dishes. It is best when used raw or lightly cooked, serves as the base for pesto sauce, and is very tasty on top of pizzas and in salads.

Chili
Penne
Arrabiata
Pasta sauces
Salsa

- **Chili** Chili is derived from dried peppers, and is available crushed or powdered. Crushed chili is used in spicy-hot dishes, and the powder is used for a more subtle spiciness. Fresh peppers can also be used for hot dishes.

chili

Stir-fry
Could be used to spice up
plain pasta sauce.
Use sparingly!

- **Chinese Five-Spice** This very different-tasting spice is a combination of several seasonings together as a powder. It is widely available in Chinese shops, though I haven't noticed it elsewhere. It's not a spice you need to replenish frequently, since it is used in very small quantities.

- **Cilantro** See coriander leaves

Fruit crumbles, Apple pie
Home-cooked black beans
Garam masala

- **Cinnamon** A versatile spice derived from the aromatic bark of a plant native to India, cinnamon is used widely in baking and desserts, as well as in savory dishes. Available as sticks, bark, or powder.

Risotto, stir-fry
Garam Masala
Baked eggplant

- **Coriander** An often-used seasoning which helps give curry its distinct flavor. Fresh ground or whole seeds provide the most noticeable flavor and can be used to spice up almost any dish.

Salsa
Burritos
Thai-Style salad

- **Coriander Leaves (cilantro)** The leaf portion of coriander has its own distinctive flavor. Cilantro is sold fresh in many stores and keeps well in fresh, cold water. It is a versatile herb used in Mexican, Thai, and Indian cuisine.

Tomato pasta sauces
Dahl (an Indian soup), Salsa
Black bean burritos
Garam masala

- **Cumin** Cumin is the pungent dried fruit of a plant related to parsley. Native to the upper Nile, it is widely used in Mexican and Indian cooking. It is available as whole seeds or powder. I like it best either used whole, or when freshly ground.

Herbs and Spices (continued)

Sample uses:

Stir-fry

- **Dill** Dill is another distinctively flavored ingredient, available as dill seed or dill weed. While dill seed is often used for pickling, dill weed is best for seasoning cooked foods or salads.

**Pasta sauces
Stir-fried vegetables
Risotto raj, Dahl**

- **Garam masala** Literally translated, garam masala means "hot spice." It is a blend made from roasted, ground spices. It can be used to add zest to almost any meal and is perfect for taking "on the road" since it's like having three or four spices in one jar. Here is my recipe for masala.

Jill's Garam masala

**¾ cup cumin seeds
⅓ cup coriander seeds
5 cinnamon sticks
⅔ cup black peppercorns
½ cup whole cardamom
⅛ cup whole cloves (optional)**

In a shallow roasting pan, spread out the spices as listed and roast for 30 minutes at 200° F. Stir the mixture once or twice and make sure the spices don't brown. When done, crush the roasted cinnamon sticks and remove the cardamom seeds from their shells (this task is a bit time-consuming).

Mix the spices in a small bowl. Grind about 1 cup at a time in a blender at high speed until the masala is a smooth powder. Pour into a bottle or jar with a tightly fitting lid. It can be stored in the freezer for months.

**Dahl soup
Garlic-butter sauce
Pasta sauces
many, more**

- **Garlic** Though garlic is really a bulb vegetable, it is best known as a seasoning. It is used extensively and is definitely best when used fresh. Garlic is also available minced in jars, flaked, as garlic powder, or garlic salt. For the strongest flavor, fresh garlic should be sautéed first, or used raw.

**Gingerbread
Dahl soup
Risotto
Stir-fry**

- **Ginger** A root native to Asia and used to flavor both sweet and savory foods. It is pungent, and can also be quite hot. Fresh root ginger is the best choice for savory dishes, while ground ginger is used in baking. Fresh ginger needs to be peeled then either sliced, finely diced, or grated.

ginger root

**Stir-fry
Dahl
Potato salad**

- **Mustard** Mustard is used in its various forms throughout these recipes. Stir-fries and Indian foods use mustard seeds which are fried with other seasonings, such as garlic. Elsewhere, mustard powder is used as is prepared mustard. Prepared mustard is the "jar" version, and can be spicy like Dijon, and English, or mild like the American variety.

9

Sample uses:

Apple crumble
Apple pie
Spice cookies
Reibekuchen
Stir-fry

"Nutmeg dreams"

oregano

Pasta sauces
Focaccia bread
Caprese salad
Stir-fry
Pizzas

Potato salad
Macaroni salad

Carrot-lentil soup
Potato salad

Herbs and Spices (continued)

• **Nutmeg** This is another spice that is used for both sweet and savory foods. It is pungent, especially freshly ground, so use it sparingly. Nutmeg is an hallucinogen, and though it would be a challenge to eat enough to produce any psychedelic effects, some people report they dream more after having nutmeg!

• **Oregano** Oregano is best known as a season-ing for Italian foods but has been used for cen-turies in Asia and Europe. It is available fresh or dried, and unlike some seasonings, it is as flavor-ful either way. It can be added to sauces while cooking or sprinkled on top before serving.

• **Paprika** This spice is made from a variety of South American peppers. Most preparations are mild or sweet, although some can be quite hot. Paprika is most often used as a garnish to add color to a dish.

• **Parsley** Fresh parsley is often used to garnish soups, side-dishes, or salads. It isn't as strong as some other herbs, but does add flavor and color when used.

Eating on the Road

(Traveling tips for athletes on the go)

Many athletes are excellent at preparing their equipment and training for events, but neglect to consider how they will meet their nutritional needs while on the road.

Just because you're in a car doesn't mean you have to eat roadkill from a hubcap! It is possible to eat well, even without relying on fast food (or is that "fat food"?).

Now you're off to the races!

As athletes, we are often required to travel to competitions. For some, this can mean an occasional weekend excursion, but for others, like professional bike racers, this may involve extensive road trips.

Many North Americans are unpleasantly surprised when they arrive in Europe to find that the food choices are very different from what they normally eat. Even while traveling within North America, there is a decided advantage to cooking your own meals rather than relying on restaurant foods.

The following pages outline these strategies for eating on the road:

(1) **The Survival Kit** • Packing light and eating healthy.

(2) **Home Cooking on the Road** • The "luxury" trail.

(3) **Cooking Without a Kitchen** • Trying to cook when stuck in a tent or hotel room.

What to pack:
• spoon
• large cup or
• small bowl
• Swiss Army Knife
(with a large blade —
along with Allen keys —
probably your handiest tool.)

Small alternatives to big meals:
muesli with yogurt,
cereal, peanut butter,
carrots, fresh fruit,
rice pudding, bread,
cheese, sandwiches.

Sports-specific meal replacement drinks are available in groceries and drug stores, and aid recovery when taken immediately after an event.

Full Meal Deal

(1) The Survival Kit

There can be times when it feels as though you are constantly hungry despite eating plenty of food. This can be caused by a diet that lacks certain nutrients. When traveling, especially to races, it is even more important than usual to eat a well-balanced diet. Filling up on plain pasta or bread and cheese might be alright for awhile, but it will eventually affect how you feel and perform.

When first racing in France, I noticed that most of the national team riders ate *a lot* of muesli and yogurt to get through the long stage races. While it's not the ideal situation, it is a viable alternative to eating large amounts of nutrient-poor foods, which fill you up without providing adequate nourishment.

You can minimize the potentially ill effects of travel by ensuring at least *some* of the food you eat is nutritional. Packing the basic utensils listed above, in the left column can make a big difference by allowing you to make a variety of healthy snacks and small meals when the need arises.

Another way to provide extra nutrients, especially while doing a stage race, is to supplement your diet with a meal replacement drink. These come in cans or powdered form and digest easily. They are particularly good after a hard effort, when it is difficult to eat right away but very important to replenish lost calories.

There are several types of meal-replacement drinks available in drugstores, and some grocery stores, but these are not usually sport-specific. Most often they are intended for hospital patients, so are very high in fat. These drinks may still be used, but should be diluted with water, juice, and/or puréed banana so that they are better suited to post-race recovery.

Canadian national team racer (and nutritionist) Kelly Anne Carter-Erdman used to pack a handheld blender when stage racing in France. This works really well for adding puréed fruit or yogurt to meal-replacement drinks, or for creating your own recovery drink.

(2) Good Home Cooking While "On the Road"

What to pack :

- Swiss Army Knife
- salt, pepper,
- favorite spices
- small cheese grater
- ingredients you use often such as cooking oil, or items which may be hard to obtain

If you are traveling for any length of time, it is easy to tire of restaurant food. Cooking while traveling is not only a good way to eat the foods you like most, and meet your nutritional needs, but it can be an enjoyable way to relax and take your mind off racing. The ideal situation is to stay in a condo or motel with kitchen-equipped units. With a few portable utensils, and seasonings, the rest is easy!

It is best to plan your meals a few days in advance so you don't have to make extra trips to the grocery store.

What to do:

- Plan a rough menu for the days you want to cook (three to five days at a time)

- Vary your meal plan according to what is available and in season

- Make a list of items you'll need for the main meals

- Add breakfast, lunch and snack foods to the list

- When buying groceries, keep in mind how long you will be at your stop

- Pack as many of the non-perishable food items as possible, to use at the next venue

A sample five-day menu and resulting grocery list:

- **Monday: Black Bean Burritos**
  tortilla shells (or flour, b. powder and shortening) black beans, salsa, avocado, rice, garlic, onion, tomato paste, vegetables of choice (broccoli, zucchini, red and green peppers, asparagus)

- **Tuesday: Pasta & Tomato Sauce**
  lentils, tomatoes, tofu, pasta, crushed tomatoes, Parmesan cheese, oregano, vegetables of choice (same as before)

- **Wednesday: Risotto Raj**
  vegetables of choice (cauliflower, carrots, mange-tout), and garam masala

- **Thursday: Pasta & Garlic Veggie Sauce**
  red pepper, mushrooms, butter, pasta

- **Friday: Pizza & Salad**
  yeast, flour, mozzarella, lettuce, leftover vegetables of choice

- **Other foods:**
  oatmeal, cereal, fresh fruit, milk, cheese, yogurt, juice, milk, oil & vinegar, fresh herbs, spices, meat or fish of choice

(3) Cooking Without a Kitchen

If you are staying in a hotel room, or camping, it is still possible to do your own cooking. As most experienced campers know, extra supplies are needed, so you can't really pack light. Even though it is inconvenient, this should be considered if you are planning a longer road trip, or are on a tight budget and still want to eat well.

Cooking in a hotel room is a pain in the butt and probably illegal, but if you are desperate for a good home-cooked meal and determined to have one, it can be done using a portable electric burner.

I've cooked in a posh Canadian hotel before a race, and just managed to escape without the maids reporting me! I had no such trouble when racing in Japan, though, so it probably depends on where you are traveling. Check ahead if possible.

Keep in mind that when refrigeration isn't an option, it is even more important to have well-planned meals. Coolers help to keep some perishable foods on hand for a short time.

What to pack for kitchen-less cooking:

- a fuel stove (camping)
- an electric burner (hotel)
- one large pot
- one frying pan (deep) with cover, if possible
- dishes and utensils as needed (plates, bowls, cups)
- Swiss Army Knife
- salt, pepper, favorite spices
- cutlery for each person
- cooler, if possible
- dish cleaning supplies
- canned or dried foods
- a small fire extinguisher?!

You loved it as a kid — love it all over again. Peanut butter on bread

Basic Nutrition

Nutrition is as much a part of race preparation as bike maintenance, but far more enjoyable! If you have a poorly maintained bike, you may be able to ride it without any problems for awhile, but eventually it will become so rundown that it will no longer function. Likewise, if your body is not nourished properly, it can reach a point where it will no longer perform.

Although it may take some time and neglect to reach an extreme situation, proper maintenance is essential. Even something as basic as not drinking enough in a race can cause a drastic change in performance.

Sports nutrition goes beyond basic survival techniques, thus giving athletes the opportunity to achieve their full potential.

Gather nutritional information from a number of sources, then find out what works best for you.

Basic nutrition is kids stuff! As easy as falling off your bicycle.

The nutrients required for good health can be divided into six main groups.

(1) Carbohydrate
Simple and Complex

(2) Protein
Amino Acids
(essential and non-essential)

(3) Fat
Saturated and Unsaturated

(4) Vitamins
Water and fat soluble

(5) Minerals
Major and trace

(6) Water
(hydration)

As a reminder:
1g CHO = 4 calories
1g Protein = 4 calories
1g Fat = 9 calories
1g Alcohol = 7 calories

How to determine the percentage of CHO, protein and fat in food and your diet:

(1) Note the total calories

(2) Multiply the grams of
•CHO by 4
•Protein by 4
•Fat by 9

(3) Divide the total calories into each of the results

The Athlete's Diet

Nutritionists recommend a varied diet as the simplest way to meet daily needs. An athlete's diet isn't much different from that of the average healthy person, except that we need to eat and drink more! When training or racing, the extra calories burned need to be replaced, while ample water is needed because of the large amount of fluid lost through sweating and breathing.

Carbohydrates (referred throughout this book as CHO), fat, and protein are the "energy-yielding" nutrients. Meeting caloric needs when training or competing can be done by increasing food portions. However, the emphasis should be on a high-CHO diet since it is the fuel of choice for intense activity.

A well-balanced diet for high-intensity endurance athletes is:

55-60% CHO + 10-15% Protein + 25-30% Fat

If you are worried about your diet, it might be worth consulting a dietitian or sports nutritionist. They usually recommend keeping a three-day food intake record, which is then analyzed for nutrient content.

Without consulting a nutritionist, you can still calculate the percentages of CHO, protein, and fat in your diet by using the formula below. I've noticed that food labels in the U.S. now include these percentages, which makes the calculations easier. It is most likely that your nutrient percentages are within the suggested range, though sometimes the amount of fat in your diet can come as a surprise!

Example Calculation (for one food item):

(1) 1 muesli bar = **170 calories**

(2) **22**g of CHO   **X 4**   =   **88 calories**
   9.25g of Protein   **X 4**   =   **37 calories**
   5g of Fat   **X 9**   =   **45 calories**

(3) **88** cal CHO   ÷170 cal =   **52% CHO**
   37 cal Protein   ÷170 cal =   **22% Protein**
   45 cal Fat   ÷170 cal =   **26% Fat**

While it's usually a bit of the naughty pleasure to "bonk" in England, it's no fun at all in North America!

Glycogen is affected by:

Genetics • We each have a limit to the amount of glycogen we can store.

Training • We can train our bodies to store more.

Diet manipulation • Carbohydrate loading lets us top up our glycogen stores to the highest possible level.

Glycogen sparing • Glucose drinks enable us to spare some glycogen for later use.

Keep in mind that it takes 2.6 grams of water to store 1 gram of CHO, so a feeling of heaviness or muscle stiffness is not uncommon when you are "carbo-loaded."

Ernst Denifl — The famous carbo-loading Austrian at the World championships, 1995.

Carbohydrate

Carbohydrate plays a crucial role in the performance of high-intensity endurance athletes such as mountain bike racers. When we ride moderately, our fat stores supply most of the fuel. Once the intensity increases, the primary fuel becomes glucose, because it is much easier and faster for the body to use.

However, stored glucose (called glycogen) is far more limited than stored fat. If the supply is exhausted and not immediately replaced, our blood sugar drops. This results in hypoglycemia, commonly referred to as "bonking." Its effects can range from blurred vision, dizziness, weakness, and fatigue to loss of consciousness or coma if not treated.

This can be avoided, or at least minimized, by carbo-loading before a race to increase the amount of glycogen. It is also possible to spare glycogen by drinking a glucose solution throughout the event. This topic is covered further in the following section on event-specific nutrition.

Getting "loaded"

Carbo-loading to build extra glycogen stores involves following a high CHO diet (70% of caloric intake) for three days leading up to a major event, while tapering training.

Alternatively, many professional racers just eat an extra large meal the night or two prior to an event. Some pros such as Ernst Denifl swear by beer as crucial extra carbs and as a digestive aid.

GIB GAS ERNST

Protein literally means "first" because of its importance as a life-giving substance.

An excess of protein could actually be detrimental because it may cause:
• increased calcium excretion
• extra workload on the kidneys
• potential dehydration due to fluid lost by the elimination of urea (a by-product of protein)

Don't worry vegetarians! A varied diet ensures that there is no special risk for protein deficiency.

Protein

Protein is a very complex structure, and is present in all our body cells. Its importance to athletes is associated with the growth and repair of muscles, tissues and blood cells, the production of enzymes and hormones, and its presence in all body cells.

While the beneficial effects of protein are obvious, it isn't true that the more protein we eat, the better. Excess protein is of no benefit since it cannot be stored and must be broken down to be used as energy or converted to fat.

Protein is found in most plant foods and all animal foods. Animal protein is considered "complete" since it contains enough of each essential amino acid. The right combination of amino acids can also be obtained by eating complementary vegetable proteins. The table below lists some of the many food combinations that make complete proteins. Food and recipe examples are included, but are only a small portion of the many possible combinations.

Complementary Vegetable Protein Table

COMBINATIONS	FOOD EXAMPLES	RECIPE EXAMPLES
Grains + Legumes	Beans and rice	Black bean burritos
	Lentil soup & rice	Lentil soup, dahl & rice
	Beans & whole wheat noodles	Minestrone soup
	Beans and bread	Black beans & cornbread
	Pasta & lentil or tofu sauce	Spaghetti sauce
	Tofu and rice	Stir-fried vegetables
Legumes + Seeds	Chickpeas and sesame seeds	Hummus and tahini
	Tofu and sesame seeds	Stir-fried vegetables
Nuts + Grains	Oatmeal and walnuts	Apple and walnut porridge
	Whole wheat and walnuts	Health-nut bread
	Peanuts and rice	Thai-style salad
Leafy green + Seeds	Broccoli and sesame seeds	Sesame fries & broccoli

Some example recipes which
can be made with meat:

Chili (con carne)
Minestrone soup
Spaghetti sauce
Lasagna
Pizza
Risotto
Burritos
Cabbage rolls
Moussaka

The Veggie View — from a
completely biased source (me).

It's quite simple; I don't like
meat, so I don't eat it.
The thought of eating animal
flesh does not excite my
appetite in the least.

Despite many expert opinions
on the subject, I don't believe
you have to eat animal
protein in order to compete at
the highest level.

Where's the beef?

You may notice when looking through the recipes in this cookbook that there are relatively few meat recipes. This is partly because I am a semi-vegetarian myself, but also because many cyclists eat less meat than the average person.

To maintain a high-carbohydrate, low-fat diet, the emphasis is often on vegetables or pasta as the bulk of a good pre-race meal, with meat as an accompaniment. Also, it is quite easy to add meat to almost any of the main-dish or pasta recipes provided. When you are adding meat to a recipe or meal it is best to find low-fat, easy-to-cook cuts which can be baked or grilled. These can be served along with a main course of high-carbohydrate foods or mixed in with an appropriate dish.

The non-veggie view
by British sports nutritionist Wilf Paish

Animal products are rich in protein, the essential amino acids that contribute to the rebuilding of our degenerative muscle protein. It is theoretically possible to make a vegetable protein complete by carefully combining vegetable sources, such as grains and legumes. The main problem is that it requires very careful thought and a very specialized knowledge of food. By and large, athletes who have to spend a considerable amount of time training for their sport do not have the time nor the expertise to do themselves justice.

So much of our body relies upon complete proteins. They are essential for the formation and efficient maintenance of our blood, muscles, and skin. They contribute to our hormone pool, as well as provide certain enzymes that are essential for our total health. The total health of the person involved in sport must be excellent; a variation of 1 percent in a performance can mean success or failure. There is no doubt in my mind that we are "what we eat," and that nutrition can give us that 1 percent that might tip the balance in our favor.

A "big" reason to consume enough fat is that it gives us a feeling of satiety, and (in theory!) prevents us from overeating.

About our nutrition expert:

Kelly Anne is a registered dietitian, and among other things, is a consultant to the Calgary Flames and the Canadian National Sport Centre. She also teaches level 4 coaching through the University of Calgary, and is a regular contributor to *Pedal* cycling magazine. Kelly Anne has made several valuable contributions to the nutrition section of this book.

Fat

Fat is the most calorie-dense of the nutrients, and provides a huge store of energy. Even though we have ample stores of fat, it is still an essential part of the diet. It is the primary source of energy for low- to mid-intensity activity and a carrier for essential nutrients.

Fat is present in so many foods that instead of making an effort to eat enough of it, we need to limit our intake to maintain a well-balanced diet.

Why a low-fat diet?
by Kelly Anne Carter-Erdman

• Dietary fats are so energy dense that they tend to fill us up easily, without leaving room to consume adequate carbohydrates.

• Excess dietary fat is stored (as body fat) four times more easily than excess carbohydrate is.

• Although we may store an abundance of energy as body fat, during aerobic exercise we will fatigue faster from running out of blood glucose than from running out of body fat as our fuel.

Most of us think of dietary fats as the butter, margarine, mayonnaise, or salad dressing that we add to our food. As an athlete, you should also be concerned with the "hidden" fat that is present in our foods. Milk products and protein-rich foods tend to be the primary sources of hidden fats. When choosing your milk products, look for either the percentage of fat or find the number of grams of fat per serving.

Keep in mind that red meat can be a nutritious, low-fat addition to your diet, as long as you avoid fatty or marbled-looking meats. Chicken and turkey are low-fat choices, and removing the skin before cooking helps to further reduce the fat content.

Kelly Anne's

Tips for Low-Fat Restaurant Meals
by Kelly Anne Carter-Erdman

May I recommend?		These are not recommended
	Appetizers	
broth-type soup (e.g. minestrone) juices, raw vegetables		nachos, potato chips, deep-fried items, cream soups
	Salads	
vegetable or fruit salads with dressing "on the side"		salads with rich dressing, croutons, egg/fish/meat salad with mayonnaise
	Meat & Alternates	
roasted, baked, broiled, boiled, trimmed of extra fat, poultry (skin removed), lemon, mustard		duck, sausage, bacon, fried/breaded items, gravy, cream sauces
	Vegetables, Potatoes & Rice	
stewed, steamed, boiled, baked, or raw		fried, buttered, creamed, scalloped, sour cream, bacon bits, fried rice
	Pasta	
any type (spaghetti, linguini, etc.) with low-fat sauces (tomato, lean meat sauce, etc.)		macaroni and cheese, lasagna, cannelloni, manicotti, pasta with cream sauce
	Breads	
whole grain breads, buns, bagels, pita bread, bread sticks, English muffins, crumpets, most crackers, pancakes, waffles, low-fat muffins		croissants, garlic toast, cheesebread/buns, Yorkshire pudding, high-fat muffins
	Desserts	
fresh fruit, fruit crisp, frozen yogurt, sherbet, sorbet, jello, rice pudding, milk pudding, angel food cake		pie, pastry, doughnuts, sweet rolls, rich desserts, chocolate, ice cream
	Beverages	
skim/no-fat milk, juices, mineral water, diet soda		alcohol, milkshakes, caffeinated beverages

Have a happy race!

Vitamins and Minerals

Vitamins and minerals are necessary for health and growth. They perform an array of functions too varied and numerous to mention. The diet is the best source of vitamins because they are present in a natural balance and therefore can be more easily absorbed.

Of importance to endurance athletes are the minerals (or electrolytes) sodium, potassium, and chloride, since they work together to maintain fluid balance. They are responsible for nerve conduction and muscle contractions. While these minerals are abundant in our diet, there is the possibility of their depletion in the extreme circumstances of heat exhaustion and dehydration. When you are racing in extremely hot and humid conditions, an electrolyte replacement drink taken in between other drinks may be of benefit.

Another mineral of note to athletes is iron, which is a trace mineral. It is required in very small amounts, but a deficiency has severe effects. Iron is needed for the production of red blood cells, which carry oxygen to our muscles and other cells. Sufficient iron stores are required for the continued production of red blood cells and can usually be maintained through diet. However, some athletes take iron supplements or a multi-vitamin with iron to reduce the risk of developing a deficiency.

Hydration

(**Note:** This topic is covered further by Kelly Anne Carter-Erdman in the section on event nutrition.)

Water comprises about 60 percent of our body weight, and muscle tissue is almost 75 percent water. It is no wonder then that adequate hydration is critical to general health and to athletic performance. The effects of fluid loss are noticeable almost immediately, and a reduction of as little as 1 percent of body weight from dehydration impairs performance.

Drink Types

When choosing race drinks, keep in mind the order of importance for replacement **(1) water, (2) carbohydrate, (3) electrolytes.**

If you want insurance against vitamin depletion, a simple "one-a-day" multi-vitamin is usually adequate.

With an unusually large fluid loss through perspiration, sodium or potassium depletion may occur, resulting in muscle cramps, nausea, vomiting and dizziness, and could lead to shock, heart palpitations, coma or even death if left untreated.

Women, vegetarians or low weight athletes are at a greater risk for developing an iron deficiency.

"Someone must have tampered with my water bottle."

Beware of mixing your drinks too strong!

Hydration through energy drinks can do the following:
• delay the point of exhaustion
• reduce fatigue
• increase performance

Event Nutrition

by Kelly Anne Carter-Erdman

Pre-event eating: The day before the event

It generally takes 24 hours to completely digest a meal.

Never venture out to expand your culinary tastes by eating unfamiliar foods the night before your event or on race day itself — you never know how your digestive system may react!

Remember to drink lots of fluids to ensure you are adequately hydrated. Limit any caffeinated or alcoholic beverages, which have dehydrating effects.

The timing of when you eat can be as important as what you eat. Before a competition, try to eat your last big meal 15 to 17 hours in advance. For example, if you race at 10:00 A.M., then have your last large meal between 5:00 and 7:00 P.M. the night before. Eating too late the night before your event may result in a "heavy" stomach sensation on race day.

Your pre-event dinner should contain large amounts of carbohydrate to contribute to your glycogen reserves. For example, 3 to 4 cups of pasta, 2 or more cups of rice, or two baked potatoes, along with lots of bread, vegetables and fruit. A moderate amount of lean protein (3 to 5 ounces) can be added to your pre-event meal. Excessive protein or dietary fat will leave you feeling lethargic come race day.

A sampling of preferred race drinks and pre-race evening meals.

Drinks	Athletes	Meals
Maxim	Caroline Alexander	Pasta or rice with chicken and vegetables
Endura Allsport & Optimizer	Sara Ballantyne	Pasta and chicken or burritos
Powdered iced tea	Laurie Brandt	Pasta primavera or black bean burritos
Apple juice and water	Elladee Brown	Rice and some veggies, pancakes (downhiller!)
Maxim plus blackcurrant	Nick Craig	Pasta with meat, water
Endura Pro Optimizer, Endura	Penny Davidson	Pasta, green salad, and maybe some cookies
Water, Coke, and/or Exceed	Susan DeMattei	Pasta with pesto sauce, bread and salad
Maxim, Red Bull, cola	Ernst Denifl	Spaghetti with tomato sauce, fish
Maxim, water or Coke	Tim Gould	Pasta or pizza with vegetables, or fish.
Maxim, sometimes Coke	Gary Foord	Pasta with veggie sauce, baked fish
Endura	Marc Kazimirski	Pasta and pepper sauce, extra spicy
Coke and water	Bill Hurley	Pasta with chicken
Carbohydrate drink	Michael Kloser	Pasta
Water	Christian Lemmerz	Pasta or rice
Glucose polymer	Ruthie Matthes	Meat or fish, rice and veggies
Water, Cytomax/High Five Pro	Deb Murrell	Pasta and vegetable sauce or rice and Indian food
emPOWERment Bars! and water	Jacquie Phelan	"Whatever I can forage"
Excel energy drink and water	Chrissy Redden	Pasta and red sauce with beef and veggies
Maxim or PSP	Sian Roberts	Pasta
Water	Alex Stieda	High complex carbo with chicken or fish
Endura/Cytomax, water	Martin Stenger	Pasta or rice, bread, and beer
Endura and Optimizer	Alison Sydor	Pasta, salad, chicken, and a small dessert
Maxim	Angela Ward	Pasta

Pre-event eating: Race day

The most immediate pre-event meal should be two to three hours before your competition. The greater the exercise intensity, the farther in advance you'll need to eat. Most mountain bike racers eat at least three hours prior to the event since it is often a sprint from the start. Every athlete and every sport is different!

With lots of carbs, you will want to consume ample fluids to ensure you are well hydrated.

Eating too soon before your competition can lead to cramps, vomiting, or other gastrointestinal upsets. This immediate pre-event meal should contain easily digestible carbohydrates with minimal fat and protein content. If you have a fast metabolism, the addition of some low-fat protein can delay hunger pangs, which otherwise may show up at the start line. Although this pre-event, high carbohydrate meal will not contribute to glycogen levels, it will provide available energy in the form of blood glucose.

The body cannot adapt to a dehydrated state, instead, your performance will inevitably suffer.

Alternatively, skipping the immediate pre-event meal will likely lead to hypoglycemia (low blood glucose), and therefore result in drawing from your limited glycogen stores sooner, thus reducing your endurance potential.

A meal replacement drink and/or a homemade shake with juice, fruit, and yogurt are ideal choices for energy within the hour before exercising.

In some situations, you may need to snack within the hour before your competition; not enough time to have a full meal. Your better choices are easily digestible complex carbohydrates (e.g. bread products) and/or fruit. Fruits are considered to be simple carbohydrates in nature, but the high fructose content causes them to be absorbed slowly, as compared to the simple carbohydrates found in "sweets".

For obvious reasons, a liquid meal will leave the stomach much faster than solid foods.

Eating during the event

Your food choices during exercise will depend on such variables as: length of activity, type of exercise, pre-event food consumption and of course, individual preference. If your event is longer than 90 minutes in duration, consumption of a sport drink or solid carbohydrate food at regular intervals while you exercise will help sustain your blood glucose levels and possibly spare using up your limited glycogen reserves. Sports drinks are the choice of mountain bike racers, since the races are shorter and it is often difficult to reach for solids while riding.

Ideally, consuming small amounts of sports drink every 15 to 20 minutes will do the trick.

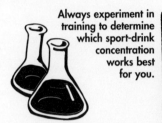

Always experiment in training to determine which sport-drink concentration works best for you.

Homemade "Greater-Aid"
4 cups fruit juice
4 cups water
¼ tsp salt

If you lack an appetite after exercising, then opt for a liquid concoction of carbohydrate and protein.

Coffee and beer after a race don't count as fluid replacement!

Healthy Food and Cooking Tips:

• prepare your own meals whenever possible

• eat raw foods and cook vegetables lightly; nutrients are lost through cooking

• whenever possible, reduce the amount of oil or butter used in recipes

• read food labels and avoid foods which have unnecessary additives

Most people can tolerate a sports drink that is anywhere from 5 to 10 percent carbohydrate concentration. If a sports drink is too concentrated, you will develop intestinal cramps and/or diarrhea. Electrolytes (sodium, potassium, and chloride) are helpful for improving carbohydrate absorption and preventing dehydration when exercising in hot and humid environments.

A homemade sports drink mixture can be created and adjusted to suit your preferences. Some individuals may find that fruit juices cause gastrointestinal cramps while exercising. A small amount of fruit juice can be used to add flavor to plain sports drinks, such as flavorless glucose polymer.

Post-event nutrition

Nutrition for recovery includes carbohydrates for replenishing your glycogen reserves and fluids to rehydrate. After your competition, the sooner you can eat, the faster you will recover. Make sure you eat within two hours after your activity.

Recent studies support the addition of small amounts of protein to your recovery meal or beverage, which seems to expedite carbohydrate repletion into glycogen. For rehydration, consume 2 cups (500 ml) of fluid for every pound of weight that you have lost.

Summary of the athlete's diet:

• Maintain a balanced diet that is approximately 60 percent CHO, 15 percent protein and 25 percent fat.
• Eat a good variety of foods for different nutrients.
• Choose fresh fruit and vegetables over prepared or snack foods.
• Avoid high-fat foods, "empty" calories and sweets in excess.
• Avoid excessive meat and protein intake.
• Choose whole grains, unrefined foods, brown rice and whole-wheat flour whenever possible.
• Listen to your body — if you have cravings for a food, it may contain something you are lacking.
• Always drink plenty of water, especially when traveling and in hot weather.
• Eat, drink, and be varied!

photo by Robert Oliver

Veggies & Main Courses

Introduction

Most of us have probably heard stories about the appalling eating habits of some professional athletes. For the most-part however, we cyclists are a health-conscious lot, and the majority of the recipes I received were well-balanced and nutritious.

The emphasis tended to be on veggie dishes, so this main course section has been combined with the vegetable section.

The first part of this chapter is a basic vegetable preparation guide with a blurb on how to prepare stir-fries. The main-course recipes take up the bulk of this chapter and are largely vegetarian. These can easily be altered to accommodate full-fledged carnivores, and there is the occasional meat dish included as well. Vegetable side dishes provide the wrap-up for this chapter.

Uses: **casseroles, stir-fries or as a side dish**
Nutrients: **niacin, vitamin C, vitamin E, vitamin K, vitamin A and folate**

Uses: **with rice, as a soup or side dish, in burritos**
Nutrients: **protein, vitamin A B-1, folate, phosphorous, potassium, iron, magnesium**

Uses: **hodge-podge, minestrone soup**
Nutrients: **potassium, folate, iron**

Uses: **pasta sauce, casseroles, stir-fry, pizza, or as a side dish**
Nutrients: **folate, vitamin C, vitamin K**

See page 143 for a broccoli cheese sauce recipe

Vegetable Preparation Guide

Vegetables are not only inexpensive and easy to prepare, but nutritious and versatile as well. This guide outlines basic preparation of most of the veggies used in this cookbook.

- **Asparagus** Tasty when steamed or boiled. Wash well and cut off the tougher bottom portions. Place in a saucepan with a small amount of boiling, salted water. Cover and cook over medium heat 10 to 15 minutes or until bottom part is tender.

- **Black beans** Soak *overnight*, rinse and boil three to four hours with seasonings. If they aren't soaked long enough, they can cause deadly gas! These are available canned, which saves time, but they aren't nearly as flavorful as the homemade variety. See recipe page 54 for the home-cooked version.

- **Broad beans** Broad beans are available frozen or garden fresh in the summer. Shell and boil in salted water for seven to ten minutes. Lima beans are similar and can be used in place of broad beans.

- **Broccoli** This very versatile and healthy vegetable is best cooked lightly to keep the nutrients intact. Wash broccoli well, after cutting off the little leafy bits and bottom of the stalk. Slice the stalk that's left and cut the florets to the desired size. Some people throw the stalk out — what a waste! Unlike broccoli florets, the peeled stalk tastes great when eaten raw.

Steamed Broccoli – "My favorite vegetable" by Sara Ballantyne

"I eat broccoli every night and throw it hot on top of a spinach salad, add it raw on top of a pizza before cooking it, or eat it by itself."

Boil water (about one-inch deep) in pot with steamer rack.
Place broccoli florets and stalks in rack.
Cover and steam for 8 to 10 minutes.

Uses: **coleslaw, stir-fries, cabbage rolls, stews, soups**

Nutrients: **vitamin K**

• **Cabbage** Makes great rolls and goes well in stir-fries. To boil, wash well and remove a few of the outer leaves. Place in a large pot of boiling, salted water and cook uncovered, until tender-crisp (about 15 minutes). Also used raw or stir-fried.

Uses: **sauces, stir-fries, salads, casseroles, or carrot pie**

Nutrients: **vitamin A, beta carotene**

• **Carrots** Carrots taste great raw, and when lightly cooked, and go well with almost any main course. To steam: wash, peel and cut the carrots. Place in a small amount of boiling, salted water and cook until tender or still slightly crunchy (tender-crisp).

Uses: **hummus, sauces, stews, and pasta dishes**

Nutrients: **protein, folate, iron, copper, magnesium**

• **Chick-peas (garbanzo beans)** To cook: soak overnight, then cook for two to three hours until tender. Canned chick-peas are much quicker, and work just as well.

Uses: **stir-fries, casseroles, pasta sauces, or side-dish**

Nutrients: **vitamin C, vitamin K, folate**

• **Cauliflower** Doesn't have a very strong flavor of its own, but it makes a tasty side dish with cheese sauce, or when stir-fried. To steam: wash and cut away the extra leaves. Either chop the cauliflower into pieces or break into florets. Boil water (about 1 inch deep) and add cauliflower. Cook, partially covered, until tender-crisp (about 15 minutes).

Uses: **pasta sauces, stir-fries, eggplant moussaka, baked, fried or deep-fried, as a side dish**

Nutrients: **vitamin C, vitamin B-12, potassium**

• **Eggplant (Aubergine)** A rich, flavorful, and substantial vegetable, eggplant soaks up flavors (*and oil*) well. To roast: slice eggplant in half lengthwise and sprinkle with olive oil. Add some seasoning, (try oregano) and place in a hot oven for about 30 minutes. Serve when tender.

Uses: **chili, soups, bean salad**

Nutrients: **copper, folate, potassium, iron**

• **Kidney beans** A sweet, distinctive-tasting bean that is easy to use in main dishes and salads. The canned variety is preferable, since kidney beans require a long time to soak and cook. Rinse before adding to recipes.

Uses: **sauces, soups, lasagna, or as a side-dish**

Nutrients: **protein, folate, manganese, potassium, phosphorous, iron, copper**

• **Lentils** Protein-rich and versatile, lentils go well in many dishes. They need to be rinsed to remove any stray stones. Pre-soaked beans cook much faster (in about 15 minutes), while unsoaked beans take up to an hour. Orange and green lentils are both used in these recipes. Orange lentils cook quicker.

Uses: **roasted or fried Avoid boiled parsnips!**

Nutrients: **vitamin C**

• **Parsnips** This was one of the rare foods I disliked; until trying them at my mother-in-laws's (British racer Tim Gould's mother)! They are excellent fried or oven roasted. To fry: Boil for five minutes, then slice parsnips into thin round pieces. Fry in butter until golden brown in color.

• **Potatoes** Potatoes are high in carbohydrates and can be prepared in many ways, including boiled, roasted, pan-fried, and of course, deep-fried. They can also be added to flour to make gnocchi pasta. A recipe for oven-roasted potatoes is found below.

Uses: **sesame fries, potato salad, Izers Epic Potatoes, reibekuchen and many more**

Nutrients: **vitamin C, potassium, the skin is high in Iron**

Oven-Roasted Parsnips or Potatoes by Mrs. Gould

Wash and peel. Cut parsnips into large pieces or potatoes into quarters. "Parboil" parsnips for five minutes in salted, boiling water; potatoes for ten minutes. Remove from the pot, drain, and place in a roasting tin. Brush with olive oil. Bake at high heat (400° F) for 45 minutes (for parsnips) to one hour (for potatoes), or until golden brown in color.

These oven-roasted potatoes or parsnips provide a delicious alternative to the boiled variety.

• **Snow peas** These are best described by the French name, mange-tout, since roughly translated it means "eat all". Unlike regular peas, the shell is also edible and tasty. They are called mange-tout in Britain (and throughout this book).

Uses: **stir-fries, salads, pasta sauces, or as a side dish**

Nutrients: **vitamin C, protein**

• **Spinach** An excellent filling for pasta or pastry, spinach makes a good salad or side dish. It needs to be washed well, since there's nothing worse than biting into the sandy grit that can be found on fresh leaves. Spinach is high in a variety of nutrients. To steam: wash well and place in a saucepan. Cook over high heat, reducing the temperature once it starts to steam. Cover and simmer until tender (five minutes).

Uses: **pasta dishes, lasagna, saag paneer, burritos, or as a side dish**

Nutrients: **vitamin A, vitamin K, iron, calcium, folate, riboflavin, beta-carotene, potassium**

• **Sweet potatoes** These make a good lunch served on their own, or with a main course. Baking them brings out their naturally sweet flavor. To bake: wash and place them whole in a moderate to hot oven (375° F) for 45 minutes. Serve with low-fat yogurt, sour cream or butter.

Uses: **can be baked or used in a stir-fries**

Nutrients: **vitamin C, vitamin A Also high in carbs**

Don't confuse sweet potatoes with yams — they *are* different! A recipe for baked yams can be found on page 149.

31

• **Tomatoes** Fresh tomatoes are used extensively throughout these recipes, as are sun-dried tomatoes. Sun-dried tomatoes are becoming increasingly popular for their distinctive taste and can be used in a variety of dishes from pasta sauce to pizza topping. They are available dried or in a jar. Jarred sun-dried tomatoes are frequently packed in oil.

The dried variety of sun-dried tomatoes have a lower fat content, and can be made at home in an oven.

"Sun" Dried Tomatoes
by Dr. Judy Kazimirski

Cut roma tomatoes in half and place cut side up on a cookie sheet. Sprinkle with coarse salt. Dry in oven at the lowest possible heat (150-200° F) for six to seven hours. Pack in sterile jars.

To reconstitute dried tomatoes place in a bowl and cover with boiled water. Cover and let sit for five minutes. Drain the liquid off and save it to add extra flavor to sauces and stews. Store extras in olive oil.

Uses: **pasta sauce, stir-fries, burritos, or in zucchini muffins**

Nutrients: **potassium**

• **Zucchini squash (courgette)** A nice additive to many dishes and even used in baking to make cakes and muffins more moist. It has a high water content, so needs to be cooked lightly for the flavor to endure the cooking process.

Stir-fried vegetables

Stir-fries are a great way to make a meal of healthy vegetables. The variations are almost endless! After the first few tries, it is worth experimenting with various spices and sauces.

To keep the veggies crisp and nutrient-rich, cook them briefly in very hot oil.

Peanut oil is best for stir-fries since it can be heated to a higher temperature.

You can reduce the amount of oil needed by using water. After heating food in hot oil, add water to create a surge of steam. This works really well for hard-to-cook veggies.

Steps for any stir-fry:

(1) **Prepare vegetables** Wash and cut to desired sizes and have ready on plates.

(2) **Heat oil** Start with 1-2 Tbsp. then add more with each new vegetable as needed.

(3) **Cook** Cook prepared veggies one at a time in the pre-heated wok, starting with ones which take longer to cook (ie. tofu, broccoli, carrots, eggplant). Add spices while tossing, and water as needed to cook through.

Suggested seasonings: black pepper, sesame seeds, sesame oil, mustard seeds, ginger, garlic, garam masala, nutmeg, cinnamon, chili, cumin powder or seeds, chinese five-spice, soy sauce, coriander, cilantro, and dill weed

(4) **Heat** Heat veggies that require only warming or slight cooking, again starting with the ones which need more time (i.e. onions, mushrooms, peppers) followed by things which require no cooking (ie. water-chestnuts, sliced almonds, sesame seeds).

(5) **Re-heat** Put everything back in the wok, to warm quickly just before serving. Add any sauces such as soy sauce and toss to mix before serving.

Main Courses

Awesome Veggie Enchiladas • Alfie's Favorite Stir-fry • Apple & Veggie Stir-fry • Cabbage Rolls • Carrot Pie • Cheesy Nut Loaf • Chicken Pilaf • Chili • Curried Tofu & Rice • Fajitas for Four • Eggplant-Faceplant Casserole • Falafel Burgers • Laurie's Black Bean Burritos • Moussaka • One-Dish Chicken Pilaf • Ratatouille Bake • Rice Medley • Rice & Chicken "a la Xander" • Risotto Raj • Saag Paneer • Sara's Black Bean Burritos • Sausage-Beef Stew • Sweet & Sour Chicken • Three-Egg Quiche • Tofu and Vegetable Burritos • Welsh Leek Flan • X-mas Nut Loaf

Canadian Track star Curt Harnett demonstrates the benefit of excess spinach intake, while Jill shows off her veggie-enhanced endurance muscles.

Awesome Veggie Enchiladas
by Deb Murrell

Enchiladas are similar to burritos, but made with a corn tortilla, rather than a flour shell. Very tasty!

1 pkg medium-firm tofu
2 Tbsp vegetable oil
3 cloves garlic, minced
1 zucchini, quartered and sliced
1 tsp chili powder
¼ cup tomato sauce

1 small onion, finely chopped
3 tomatoes, chopped

8-10 corn tortillas

Enchilada sauce
(see recipe page 34)

1 cup grated cheese
(mozzarella, edam or cheddar)

Heat oil in a large frying pan.
Crumble in tofu and toss with the garlic until lightly browned.
Stir in the zucchini and cook until it is almost tender.
Add the tomato sauce and season with chili powder, salt, and pepper.
Chop the onions and tomatoes and have ready on a plate.
Heat each corn tortilla in a frying pan, or over an open flame, until it is soft and flexible. Fill with the vegetable mixture, onions, and tomatoes.
Fold in half and place in a large 2" deep pan.
Cover with enchilada sauce and grated cheese.
Heat through in a 350°F oven for 20-30 minutes.
Serve warm with rice, beans, salsa, sour cream and guacamole.

Variations: You can replace the zucchini with a vegetable of choice. I often use cooked spinach, eggplant, or broccoli. Chopped lettuce and/or black beans (with tomatoes and onions) are other alternative fillings.

Alfie's Favorite Stir-Fry

This is the stir-fry I make most often. It can be made with the vegetables or meat of your choice.

1 package firm
or smoked tofu
1 large broccoli, chopped
2 medium carrots, sliced
snow peas (mange-tout)
5-10 mushrooms
vegetable oil
½-1 tsp sesame oil
water, soy sauce
3 cloves garlic, finely
1 small onion, chopped
black pepper, ground
cumin, chili powder
2 tsp fresh ginger, finely
chopped or grated
pinch of nutmeg

Drain the tofu and cut into pieces.
Fry in 2 Tbsp vegetable oil and sesame oil with cumin and chili powder.
Cover with 2 tsp soy sauce and remove when the sauce has been absorbed or fried off.
Add the carrots and toss with diced ginger and a pinch of nutmeg. Remove carrots and set aside.
Heat the broccoli, add water and cover until tender-crisp, then remove broccoli.
Sauté the mushrooms and snow-peas.
Add the garlic and onion and sauté briefly.
Put everything back into the wok or pan, add bean sprouts, sliced almonds and soy sauce to taste.
Toss well, and heat through.

Serve warm with rice and extra soy sauce.

Spicy Enchilada Sauce

For veggie enchiladas. Can also be used for burritos.

1 Tbsp. vegetable oil
2 cloves garlic, minced
1 small onion, finely chopped

Fry onion and garlic until onion is soft.
Add the seasonings and tomato sauces blend well.
Cook over low to medium heat for about 15 minutes.
Season with salt as needed.

2 tsp ground cumin
2 tsp chili powder,
more to taste

Can be used over enchiladas, or burritos.
Also provides some extra zap to plain rice.

1 can tomato sauce
1 can tomato paste

¡HEY GRINGO!
THINK YOU'RE
TOUGH ENOUGH?

34

Angela is a talented young cyclist who has been racing for six years. She has begun to compete on the World Cup circuit and came in third at the British National Championships in 1994. Her other sports and interest include weights, running, kite flying, rock climbing, films and music.

Angela Ward

Derbyshire, England

Favorite foods: Melon, bananas, chicken, pasta, chilies, and rice pudding
Pre-race evening meal: Pasta
Pre-race breakfast: Cereal, then power bars, apricots.
Race drinks and food: Maxim drink and bananas
Vitamin supplements: Multi-vitamins
Nutritional hints: "Lots of training means you eat loads. Have variety — don't just eat pasta day after day. Eat fresh fruit and vegetables. They are very refreshing and stop you wanting to eat "junk" food in between meals

Pro·file

Apple & Veggie Stir-Fry
by Angela Ward

Here's another variation of stir-fry that makes a really tasty vegetable dish or main course.

2 large leeks
4 sticks celery
2 large courgettes (zucchini)
1 red pepper
2 Tbsp olive oil
1 garlic clove
2 Tbsp medium curry paste
(or 2 tsp curry powder)
1 level Tbsp ground ginger
1 Tbsp honey
2 crisp eating apples
2 oz (½ cup) unsalted cashew nuts
1 lemon

Slice the leeks, celery and courgettes (zucchini), and finely chop the red pepper.
Heat oil and cook crushed garlic for a few seconds then add vegetables and cook for 10 minutes.
Add curry paste (or powder mixed with water), ginger, honey, and 3 Tbsp water and stir until smooth.
Roughly chop the apples.
Add the apples to the pan with cashew nuts and plenty of seasoning.

Cook for a further 5 minutes until veggies are cooked, but still slightly crunchy.

Add squeezed lemon juice just before serving.

Cabbage Rolls

Another healthy "full-meal-deal." These can be made in advance.

Rolls:
1 large cabbage
1 package medium-firm tofu, spicy fried
1 cup cooked brown rice
½ cup chopped walnuts
1 medium apple, diced
salt and pepper to taste
¼ tsp cinnamon
salt to taste

Cook cabbage leaves in boiling, salted water for 7-10 minutes to soften. Remove and drain.
For the rolls:
Finely chop or coarsely blend the walnuts.
Mix the cooked tofu, rice, apple, walnuts and seasonings in a bowl.
For each roll, gently remove one cabbage leaf, then fill with the cooked mixture and wrap well. Hold together with toothpicks.

Sauce:
1 onion
3 garlic cloves
2 cans tomatoes (large)
1 small can tomato paste
2 tsp oregano
1 Tbsp ground cumin
salt and pepper to taste

For the sauce:
Sauté onions, garlic and spices in a large pot, then add tomato sauce and tomato paste.
Season with salt and pepper.

Gently place rolls into sauce and simmer on low heat for 1 hour. Serve with rice.

Top Tip by Dr. Judy Kazimirski: As an option, the cabbage rolls can be layered in a casserole dish with sauerkraut and brown sugar.

Carrot Pie
by Sian Roberts

This Welsh dish is healthy and hearty.

1 portion wholemeal pastry (recipe page 90)
¼ cup (2 oz) butter
2½ cups (10 oz) onion, chopped
3 cups (10 oz) carrots, grated
1 cup (4 oz) parsnips, grated

large pinch of mixed herbs
3 Tbsp whole-meal flour
2 tsp yeast extract (Marmite or Vegemite)
1 tsp tomato purée (paste)
black pepper to taste
4 tsp water

Line a 9-inch pie dish with half of the pastry shell (pie crust).

Melt the butter and gently fry the onion.

Add the carrots and parsnips and fry gently for a further 10 minutes or so, stirring continuously.

Stir the herbs, flour, yeast extract, tomato purée, water, and pepper into the carrot mixture.

Pour into the pie dish and top with the rest of the pastry.

Bake at 400° F (Gas mark 6) for 35-40 minutes.

"Fast Eddy," as Mr. Foord is sometimes called, has been mountain bike racing for just four years after a background in road racing. He made his mark quickly on the World Cup circuit with a brilliant win at the Mammoth World Cup race in 1994 and 4th place overall in the 1995 World Cup series. His other interests include road racing, cyclo-cross, running and classic cars.

Gary Foord

Staffordshire, England

Pre-race evening meal: Pasta and pizza
Pre-race breakfast: Muesli, toast, coffee
Race drinks and food: Maxim, sometimes cola
Vitamin supplements: Multi-vitamins
Nutritional hints: "Everything in moderation, except after a race — then everything in excessive amounts!"

Cheesy Nut Loaf & Tomato Sauce
by Gary Foord

Special thanks to Karen Dreaves for this delicious and easy to make nut loaf.

Ingredients	
1 Tbsp oil	
1 medium onion, chopped	
1 medium green pepper, chopped	
1 tomato, chopped	
1 cup roasted unsalted cashew nuts	
1 cup blanched almonds	
1 carrot, grated	
1 cup cooked brown rice	
¾ cup grated cheddar cheese 1 egg, lightly beaten	

Tomato sauce:
1 Tbsp olive oil
6 medium tomatoes, chopped
¼ cup water

Oil a loaf pan and line with greaseproof paper. Heat oil, then cook onion, pepper, and tomato on low heat for 4 minutes.

Blend or process cashews and almonds until finely chopped. Mix onion mixture with other ingredients and press into loaf pan.

Bake for 40 minutes in moderate oven (350° F) or until brown.

Served warm with tomato sauce.

Tomato sauce:
Heat oil, add tomatoes and cook on low heat for 10 minutes. Blend with water until smooth, and then strain. Serve over nut loaf.

Note: Bread sauce (recipe page 144) also goes well with this loaf.

Chicken Pilaf
by Angela Ward

A nice, light chicken and rice dish.

1 onion **1 Tbsp olive oil**	Fry onion in oil until golden.
1¼ cup (8 oz) long grain or basmati rice	Add rice, fry for a minute, turning all the time.
2 cups (1 pint) water	Pour in water, bring to boil. Cover pan, lower heat, and simmer for 15 minutes
8 oz cooked chicken **¼ cup (2 oz) raisins** **grated rind of orange** **½ cup (4 oz) skinned** **and chopped tomatoes** **⅓ cup (1 oz) blanched** **almonds, chopped**	until rice is cooked and most of the water absorbed. Add all remaining ingredients and continue to simmer until rice has absorbed the liquid. Serve immediately.

Chili
by Gary Foord

Gary says, "I have this whenever my fridge needs cleaning out! You can make it with just about any vegetable."

1 package tofu, crumbled or Quorn* (see note below)
vegetable oil
3-4 cloves garlic, minced or grated
fresh chili peppers
1 large onion, chopped
veggies of choice (broccoli, potatoes cauliflower, whatever you have on hand.)
1 can kidney beans, rinsed, and/or 1 can chick peas
1-2 cans whole tomatoes
1 Tbsp chili powder
2 tsp ground cumin
salt and black pepper to taste

In a large pot heat the oil and stir-fry the crumbled tofu or Quorn.*
When it starts to brown, add the garlic and onions. Fry for a few minutes, then add vegetables and diced fresh chili peppers (start with two small peppers).
When they have heated, add the cans of tomatoes and the remaining spices.
Cook on medium heat until the vegetables are almost tender, then add the beans, reduce heat and simmer.
Check seasoning and add extra chili powder and cumin as well as salt and pepper as needed.
For a much spicier chili, add crushed chilies or extra fresh chili peppers — but only a little at a time!
Serve hot. Goes well with rice.

*Note: Quorn is a British product made from textured vegetable protein (TVP). Tastes great and cooks quickly.

Curried Tofu & Rice
by Marc Kazimirski

A great meal for when you're in the mood for some spice! Thanks to Kate McLarty as well for this recipe.

1 package firm tofu
1½ Tbsp peanut butter
1 tsp oil (regular or sesame)
3 Tbsp Tamari or soy sauce
1 Tbsp green onion, minced
1 Tbsp honey
1 Tbsp curry powder
pepper to taste

Press water out of the tofu and cut into small cubes.

Mix all ingredients except the tofu and rice to make a marinade.
Add the tofu cubes and let sit for to 1 hour.
Reserve remaining marinade.

Bake cubes on a cookie tray at 350° F for 5-10 minutes.

Blend rice with tofu and reserved marinade; serve alone or with a vegetable stir-fry.

1½-2 cups cooked long grain white or basmati rice

Eggplant-Faceplant Casserole

This side dish is a low-fat way to serve eggplant.

1 large eggplant
1 Tbsp olive oil
3 cloves garlic
1 medium onion, diced
5-10 mushrooms, sliced
1 tsp garam masala
½ tsp cumin seeds
½ tsp chili powder
1 red pepper, diced
1 can yellow corn
¾ cup tomato sauce
¼ cup pine nuts
salt and pepper to taste

Place whole eggplant on a lightly oiled sheet.
Bake at 425° F until tender (about 30 minutes).
When eggplant is cool, cut to bite-sized pieces.

Fry the onion and garlic in oil and add the spices and mushrooms when the garlic starts to brown.
Cook for another minute.
Add the eggplant, corn and red pepper.
Pour the tomato sauce over the vegetables and mix well. Add the pine nuts.
Season with salt and pepper to taste.

Transfer to an ovenproof dish and bake at 350° F for 20 minutes. Serve with rice or pasta and plain yogurt if desired.

Pro·file

Martin has been racing for 15 years, duking it out with the best in the world and occasionally surprising everyone (including himself), with an awesome result! Martin loves to cook, and meals at his place are always excellent. His hobbies include ice-hockey, telemark skiing/touring, good beer and sex. (Or is that good sex and beer?)

Martin Stenger
Salt Lake City, Utah

Favorite foods: Mexican, Italian, and Japanese, fajitas and veggie sushi (Martin makes killer sushi!)
Pre-race evening meal: Pasta/rice and bread, with beer (of course)
Pre-race breakfast: Toast, jam, juice and fruit
Race drink & Food: Endura or Cytomax, water
Nutritional hints: "Don't take racing too seriously There is a lot more to life than miracle supplements and crusher races."

Fajitas for Four (bike racers!)
by Martin Stenger

Another delicious dish, this can be made with meat of your choice or alternatives as suggested.

2 cups cubed (½"x½") chicken, beef, or lean pork
Option: 1 package tofu or tempeh, cubed
3 peppers: red, yellow, and green
2 Anaheim peppers (mild)
½ large white onion or 6 green onions, chopped
2-3 cloves garlic, crushed
½ tsp ground cumin
½ tsp cayenne pepper
½ tsp salt
flour or corn tortillas
rice, lettuce, tomatoes, and black beans for serving

Put some rice on to cook and prepare the lettuce, tomatoes, and black beans for serving.

Sauté meat, onions, and garlic until done. If using tofu, sauté, then set aside to mix last.

Dice the peppers and remove seeds. Add peppers, chilies, spices, and salt to taste.

Stir constantly on high heat.

Warm tortillas in oven. Make into burritos (flour tortilla) or tacos (corn tortilla) by filling each shell with cooked filling, lettuce, and tomatoes.

Serve with black beans, rice, and salsa on the side. "Get it in ya!"

Falafel Burgers
by Alison Sydor

Falafel burgers are a good source of vegetable protein as well as being tasty and filling. Makes four burgers.

19oz/540ml can chick peas
4 cloves garlic
1 egg
parsley, minced
3 green onions
¼ cup tahini
¼ cup dry bread crumbs
1 tsp ground cumin
1½ tsp basil, dried
1½ tsp thyme
1½ tsp turmeric
¼ tsp fresh ground pepper
⅛ tsp salt
1 Tbsp vegetable oil
4 pitas

In a food processor or blender, combine chick peas and garlic.
Process until smooth. Add egg and mix.
Transfer to medium bowl and stir in parsley, onion, tahini, bread crumbs, and spices.
Shape into 4 patties. In a large non-stick skillet, heat oil over medium to high heat and cook patties for 5-7 minutes per side.
Cut pita in half and put ½ burger in each side.

Top as desired with tomatoes, sprouts, lettuce, etc., and tahini sauce. Tahini sauce is important because the burgers tend to be dry.

See recipe for tahini sauce below.

Tahini Sauce
by Alison Sydor

Goes with the falafel burgers. Can also be used as a salad dressing or dip.

---

1 cup low-fat yogurt
2 Tbsp tahini
2 Tbsp parsley
1 Tbsp lemon juice
2 green onions, minced
1 clove garlic, minced
½ tsp cumin
⅛ tsp black pepper
pinch cayenne pepper
(optional)
pinch salt

In a jar, combine all ingredients.

Shake well and spread on burgers, along with other toppings of choice.

"There's nothing better than a good cinnamon bun and good cup of coffee."
— Alison

Pro·file

Laurie has been a professional mountain bike racer for five years, and is well-known on the World Cup and NORBA circuits. She excels at climbing, and rides well at altitude. Her other interests include vegetable gardening, hiking, tinkering with and building things around the house. She is also quite interested in the preparation and consumption of good food!

Laurie Brandt

Louisville, Colorado

Favorite foods: Wholegrain pancakes, stir-fry vegetables with brown rice, cantaloupe, black bean burritos, romaine salads, bean soups, stews with dense breads.

Pre-race evening meal: Black bean burritos or pasta primavera

Pre-race breakfast: Wholegrain pancakes or oatmeal and cream of wheat mixed together.

Race drinks and food: Shaklee Performance and Carbo Crunch bars during rides and Shaklee Physique for recovery.

Nutritional Supplements: Vita-Lea multi-vitamin, calcium, Alf-alfa, Formula I

Laurie's Black Bean Burritos
by Laurie Brandt

Here is another recipe for black bean burritos, different and delicious!

**black beans (cooked or canned)
cumin powder
(1 tsp per 2 cups beans)
1 bunch cilantro
1 large tomato, chopped
1 onion, chopped
1 can chopped green peppers or salsa**

**1¼ cup cheese, grated
black olives, sliced**

whole wheat tortillas

Heat black beans and cumin together in a saucepan.

Rinse cilantro well, remove leaves and discard stems.

Chop tomato, onion, and green peppers. (Either green peppers, salsa, or tomatillo salsa works great.)

Heat tortillas in a skillet.

Pile the ingredients in a warmed tortilla, fold it and eat!

42

Mixed Vegetable Balti

This flavorful curry dish has a tomato base and makes a nice spicy meal.

Sauce:
3 Tbsp oil
4 cloves garlic, minced
2 onions, chopped
1" piece ginger root, grated
seeds of 5 cardamom
5 whole cloves (optional)
1 Tbsp each:
coriander, cumin, paprika, turmeric, cinnamon, chili powder
1 large can chopped tomatoes
2½ cups vegetable stock
juice and rind of 1 lemon
fresh chili peppers (optional)
vegetables of choice

Heat oil and fry the garlic, onions, and ginger for 5 minutes.
Add the spices and fry another minute.
Stir in the tomatoes, vegetable stock, lemon juice, and pared rind of lemon.
Fry for a few minutes, then add vegetables of choice (such as potatoes, cauliflower, and broccoli) to the sauce.
Bring to a boil, then reduce heat and simmer for 30 minutes.
Remove lemon rind and simmer until vegetables are tender.
Serve warm in bowls over basmati rice.

Variation: Add cooked or canned chick-peas, beans, or peas and heat through before serving. Add fresh chili pepper for a spicy Balti.

Moussaka

This classic Greek dish is made with eggplant, to make it rich and flavorful.

4 medium potatoes, cut into thin slices
2 eggplants, sliced about ⅛" thick
2 Tbsp olive oil
1 large onion
2 cloves garlic
1 can tomato sauce, 8 oz
1 tsp oregano
salt and pepper to taste

Bechamel Sauce
(recipe page 144)
½ cup grated cheddar cheese (optional)

Slice the potatoes and cook in boiling, salted water until softened but not fully cooked.
Fry the eggplant slices in the oil until almost softened.
Add the onion and garlic to sauté, and sprinkle with oregano, salt, and pepper. Mix in the tomato sauce.

In a large casserole dish assemble in alternating layers: potato, tomato sauce, eggplant, and tomato sauce, finishing with potato.

Cover with bechamel sauce and grated cheese.

Bake at 350° F for 1 hour.

43

One-Dish Chicken Pilaf
by Kelly Anne Carter Erdman

A quick, one-dish meal.

2 chicken breasts (boneless and skinless)	Prepare all the veggies.
½ cup brown rice	Cut the chicken into 1½" pieces.
1½ cup water or vegetable stock	Sauté the chicken and onion in oil for a few minutes.
2 bay leaves	Add all the other ingredients to the large saucepan.
½ cup frozen peas	
1 stalk celery, diced	

**2 chicken breasts
(boneless and skinless)
½ cup brown rice
1½ cup water or
vegetable stock
2 bay leaves
½ cup frozen peas
1 stalk celery, diced
1 carrot, diced
2 tomatoes, cut in wedges
½ onion, diced
⅓-½ cup raisins or currants
½ tsp allspice
1 Tbsp olive oil**

Prepare all the veggies.
Cut the chicken into 1½" pieces.
Sauté the chicken and onion in oil for a few minutes.
Add all the other ingredients to the large saucepan.

Bring to a boil, then reduce heat and simmer for 40-45 minutes, until the rice is done.

Remove bay leaves and serve.

Ratatouille Bake
by Mrs. C. Gould

This is one of the recipes Mrs. Gould created when she found her son had turned semi-vegetarian!

**3 cloves garlic, 1 onion
1 medium zucchini (courgette)
1 eggplant (optional)
1 red pepper
1 green pepper
1 can chopped tomatoes
pine nuts
salt and pepper**

Cut the zucchini into medium-sized pieces.
Slice the eggplant and peppers.
Sauté the garlic and onion.
Add the zucchini, eggplant, peppers, and seasoning, and cook for a few minutes.

Add the tomatoes and simmer for 20 minutes.

**Crumble topping:
¾ cup (2oz) whole wheat
bread crumbs
1 cup grated cheddar cheese
½ cup pumpkin seeds**

Place in a pan and cover with bread crumbs and cheese.
Sprinkle the pumpkin seeds on top.

Bake at 375° F for 20 minutes.

Caroline has been racing only six years, and has made her mark on the World Cup circuit. She is Britain's top rider and among other great results, finished second overall in the 1994 World Cup Series and was crowned European champion in 1995. Her other interests include running and socializing.

Lake District, England

Caroline Alexander

Favorite foods: Muffins, toast, flap-jacks, pasta, vegetables, and chicken or tuna
Pre-race evening meal: Pasta or rice with chicken and vegetables.
Pre-race breakfast: Cereal, toast, bagel and Powerbar.
Race drinks and food: Maxim
Vitamin supplements: Multi-vitamin, iron and vitamin C
Nutritional hints: "The tannin in tea and coffee destroys the nutrients in your food, so should be avoided at all times."

Pro·file

Rice and Chicken a la Xander
by Caroline Alexander

This chicken dish is quick and easy to make.

Lundberg wild blend brown rice (or ¼ cup wild rice per cup of brown rice) garlic salt fresh basil chicken breasts (chopped into bite-size pieces)	Cook rice according to package instructions (or use your own mix of brown and wild rice, bring to a boil and cover and simmer for an hour). Heat some water in a frying pan and add garlic salt and fresh, chopped basil. Add chicken and cook, turning frequently for 15 or so minutes. Do not allow water to boil dry.
carrots broccoli sweetcorn (corn) mange-tout (snow peas) mushrooms	Add carrots and broccoli and cover pan with lid to allow vegetables to steam. Finally add sweetcorn, mange-tout, mushrooms and any seasoning you like (oregano is a good one).
pepper to taste seasonings of choice	Serve with rice.

45

Rice Medley
by Ruthie Matthes

"Delete or add the flax seed oil if you like. It is key to me, I like the flavor and don't have to eat again in 15 minutes."

1 cup brown rice
2½ cups water
veggies of choice, raw or cooked
1 Tbsp flax seed oil
sun-dried tomatoes
feta cheese
olives
fresh basil to taste
beans (optional)

To prepare rice: boil water, add rice and let water rise to a boil, then cover and simmer for 1 hour.

Prepare vegetables of choice.

In a bowl mix all ingredients in amounts desired.

Toss lightly and serve warm.

Risotto Raj

This is a quick way to prepare a curry-style rice meal.

3 Tbsp vegetable oil
1 onion, sliced
3 cloves garlic, finely chopped
½-inch ginger, grated
1 Tbsp garam masala (recipe page 9)
1 cup rice, rinsed
vegetables of choice (broccoli, cauliflower)
salt and pepper
1 cup water or vegetable stock
1 cup chopped tomatoes or tomato sauce

3 Tbsp chopped fresh cilantro

Heat the oil and fry the onions and garlic for 1 minute.
Stir in the garam masala and ginger.
Add the rice and stir again.

Add the vegetables and cook for 2 minutes.
Add the water or stock and tomato sauce.

Cook over medium heat for 10 minutes.
Season with salt and pepper.

Cover and simmer until all the liquid is absorbed, stirring occasionally.
If the rice isn't tender yet, add more water and let it absorb.
Keep covered and sprinkle with cilantro when ready to serve.

Saag Paneer

This simple East Indian dish is one of my all-time favorites. I've sampled it in many restaurants, but the homemade is just as good, if not better.

2 bunches spinach
salt to taste
2 Tbsp ghee or vegetable oil
1 onion, finely chopped
or grated
1-inch piece ginger, grated
½ tsp chili powder
(more to taste)
1 tsp cumin seeds, ground
½ tsp turmeric powder
8 oz paneer
(Indian cheese)
2 Tbsp tomato paste

Wash the fresh spinach well. Cook in a medium pot with a small amount of water. Add salt to taste.

Heat oil in a frying pan and cook the onions and garlic briefly. Add ginger and spices and fry for a few more minutes. Add spinach to this mixture. Cut the paneer into ½-inch cubes.
Gently toss paneer with the cooked spinach mixture and tomato paste.
Serve with rice and another curry dish, if desired.

Notes: Frozen spinach can also be used. Two cups of frozen is the approximate equivalent to 2 bunches.
For homemade paneer, see recipe on page 48.

Sara's Black Bean Burritos
by Sara Ballantyne

Sara says, "Every time I make this it turns out different. Potatoes can be added inside as well." Awesome!!

garlic cloves, minced
1 onion, finely chopped
cumin powder
canned black beans
fresh ground pepper

whole-wheat tortillas
sharp cheddar cheese
fresh tomatoes
non-fat plain yogurt
alfalfa sprouts
salsa

Sauté as many garlic cloves as desired in olive oil with onion.
After a few minutes, add black beans, a lot of cumin, and a sprinkle of black pepper.
Simmer for awhile to blend flavors.

Heat up tortillas in oven, toaster, or over an open flame.
Lay cheese on heated tortilla.
Add hot beans followed by fresh tomatoes, sprouts, and non-fat plain yogurt. Top with salsa.

Variations: For extra protein, cook and add chicken or tofu.

Homemade Paneer

Paneer is a plain type of East Indian cheese. It's high in protein, has a very nice texture and mild flavor.

---

4 cups milk
juice of 1 lemon

You won't be needing a grater for this cheese!

Bring milk to a near boil, while stirring continuously.
When it starts to bubble, add lemon juice and remove from heat.
Stir gently until all the milk curdles.
Let sit for 15 minutes while the curd separates from the whey.
Strain through 3 layers of cheesecloth, squeezing out as much whey as possible.
The curds are now like cottage cheese and could be used as is, if desired.
For a firm paneer press into a rectangular shape (still in the cheesecloth) and cover with a very heavy object to flatten it for an hour.

When ready, cut into cubes and use in recipes.

Sausage-Beef Stew
by Chrissy Redden

"Good with crusty bread, salad and beer. Especially good after a long winter ride."

---

6 sweet Italian sausages
1lb stewing beef, cut in 1" cubes
1 large onion, sliced
1 clove garlic, minced
2 medium green peppers
4 potatoes, peeled and cut
turnip or sweet potato (optional)
2 cans red kidney beans
1 tsp basil
½ tsp salt, ¼ tsp pepper
2 beef bouillon cubes in 1 cup boiling water

beer (optional)

Brown sausages well. Cut each link in thirds and place in 3-quart casserole dish.
Brown beef cubes in same frying pan or skillet.
Cook onion and garlic until tender, add green pepper and cook one minute longer.
Turn into casserole dish.
Add potatoes, drained kidney beans, turnip, and sweet potatoes (if desired).

Sprinkle with seasonings and mix lightly.
Add bouillon mixture.
Cover and bake at 350° F for 1 hour 15 minutes (or until beef and potatoes are tender).

Add beer for an interesting flavor!

Kelly Anne raced for ten years, eight of which were with the Canadian national team. She holds multiple national champion titles and was top five in the world championships. Although Kelly Anne no longer races, she still gets plenty of training by riding through the Rocky Mountains of Banff with her daughter, Adrianne, in a Burly™ trailer behind her.

Kelly Anne Banff, Alberta
Carter Erdman

Favorite foods: "I like just about anything."
Pre-race evening meal: Baked potatoes with cheese.
Race drinks and food: Always a sports drink, sometimes a jam sandwich with butter on it.
Nutritional hints: "Some racers need a little fat and protein with their pre-race meal. It works well for me, because otherwise I'd get hungry during the race."
Vitamin supplements: Multi-vitamin, iron

Sweet & Sour Chicken
by Kelly Anne Carter Erdman

A simple and tasty chicken dish.

Sweet and sour marinade:

½ cup orange juice
2 Tbsp soy sauce
3 Tbsp orange/lemon marmalade
½-1 tsp ground ginger or
1 Tbsp grated ginger root

4 chicken breasts, boneless and skinless

Blend together first four ingredients.
Place chicken breasts in a lightly greased baking dish and prick all over with a fork.
Pour marinade over chicken breasts.
Try to marinate for at least 2 hours, turning chicken every 30 minutes.

Bake at 350° F for 30 minutes, turning chicken once or twice and spooning sauce on top.

Serve with rice or pasta.

Spanish Tortilla

This spanish dish is like an omelet with potatoes. Lots of carbs — makes a great lunch.

2 Tbsp vegetable oil
2 to 3 medium potatoes, sliced (about 2 cups)
1 onion, sliced

½ cup cooked spinach
6 eggs
salt and pepper
grated cheese (optional)

salsa to serve

Heat oil in a large frying pan over medium heat. Toss in the potatoes and cook until golden and tender, about ten minutes.

Add the onions and continue to cook for three minutes.

Stir in the cooked spinach, then pour in the beaten eggs.

Add salt and pepper and let this cook for five minutes, shaking the pan occasionally.

To cook through, place a plate over the tortilla and gently flip the frying pan over.

Slide the tortilla back into the frying pan, and cook for another three minutes.

Alternatively, to cook the other side, you can place the pan under a hot grill for three minutes.

Add cheese last and allow to melt.

Serve with lots of spicy salsa, and sour cream if desired.

Three Egg Quiche

This dish is surprisingly light and very tasty.

9-inch pie shell (recipe page 90)
1 cup cooked vegetables: (½ cup each: broccoli, zucchini, carrots, or vegetable of choice)
2 green onions, chopped

3 eggs
2 cups milk
½ tsp salt
black pepper
1 cup cheddar cheese, grated

Prepare the pie shell as per recipe.

Cook the vegetables, except for the green onions, until almost tender.

Beat the eggs and add the milk.
Mix in the vegetables, onions, seasonings, and cheese.

Pour into unbaked pie shell.
Bake at 400° F for 45 minutes.
Let stand 15 minutes before serving.

Variations: This quiche can also be made with plain or smoked salmon. Sun-dried tomatoes are another tasty option, though ¼ cup would be plenty.

Tofu and Veggie Burritos

These burritos are a full-meal-deal when served with rice, being high in protein and low in fat.

**Spicy fried tofu
(recipe page 58)
1½ cups chopped broccoli
1 zucchini quartered then
sliced medium thickness
2 ripe tomatoes
1 medium onion, finely
chopped
whole wheat or plain tortillas
(recipe page 52)
1 cup tomato purée/sauce
1-2 tsp chili powder
salt and pepper to taste
1 cup grated cheese**

**Variations: asparagus
or cauliflower**

Lightly steam the broccoli pieces, and add the zucchini when the broccoli is almost soft.
Chop the fresh tomatoes and onions.
Have all ingredients ready and place in the middle of each tortilla shell: 1 large spoonful each of veggies, tofu, tomato and onion. Make sure they are not too full to close over!
Roll securely and place in a large, 2-inch deep pan. Mix chili powder with the tomato sauce and season with salt and pepper.
Cover the burritos with the tomato sauce mixture. Top with grated cheddar or other cheese of choice, and bake at 350° F for 15 minutes.

Note: For an extra spicy sauce, try store-bought enchilada sauce. Or, try the enchilada sauce recipe on page 34.
You can also vary the fillings, using your own favorites.

Welsh Leek Flan
by Sian Roberts

A traditional Welsh dish — always a treat.

**1 portion (10 oz)
wholemeal pastry crust
(recipe page 90)**

**2 large leeks, sliced
2 Tbsp (1 oz) butter
3 free-range eggs
½ cup (6 fl oz) milk
pinch of black pepper
pinch of mixed herbs
1 cup (6 oz) cheese, grated**

Line a 9-inch flan tin with pastry.

Fry the leeks in the butter.
Beat together the eggs, milk, herbs, and pepper.

Put half the cheese on the base of the pan, spread the leeks on top, then the rest of the cheese.

Pour the egg mixture onto the filling.
Bake at 400° F (Gas mark 6) for about 30-35 minutes, or until filling is set.

51

Tortillas (for Burritos)

This basic recipe makes enough tortillas to serve up to 20 people! You can make the full batch or a quarter of it as below.

Full recipe:

8 cups flour
3¼ cups water
1 Tbsp salt
1Tbsp baking powder
1 cup shortening

¼ recipe:

2 cups flour
¾ cup water
1½ tsp salt
1½ tsp baking powder
¼ cup shortening

Combine the dry ingredients and mix in the shortening. Add water to make a soft dough and form into a ball.

If possible, refrigerate for 1 hour to make the dough easier to work with later.

Break off a small piece at a time from the large ball and form it into a smaller ball. Roll out on a well-floured surface into a large thin circle.

Fry each tortilla in a hot, non-stick frying pan, or just enough oil to prevent the tortilla from sticking to the pan.

Once you see bubbles appear, turn it over and fry the other side until lightly browned.

Keep warm until ready to serve, unless they will be reheated later.

X-mas Nut Loaf

This healthy and sumptuous feast has been my contribution to Christmas dinner for the last few years.

Filling:

1 cup brown rice, cooked
¼ cup wild rice, cooked
1 package medium-
firm tofu, crumbled
olive oil
2 cloves garlic, finely chopped
1 onion, finely chopped
2 celery stalks
1 cup chick peas,
cooked or canned
½ cup chopped walnuts
½ cup pine nuts
savory and sage
2 tsp garam masala
(optional)
1 portion of "puff" pastry
(recipe page 113)

Cook rice and set aside.
Fry tofu in 2-3 Tbsp olive oil until lightly browned.
Add garlic, onion, and celery and lightly sauté.
Purée chick peas in a blender, or mash well.
Mix rice, tofu, veggies, and nuts in a large bowl.
Add puréed chick peas and mix well.
Add spices and adjust seasonings to taste.
Make pastry as per recipe (p.113) and roll out into a large rectangle a little smaller than the average cookie sheet. Trim excess dough.
Spoon prepared mixture onto the middle of the pastry. Fold over and seal edges. Place on a cookie sheet and flip so that the seam is on the bottom.
Decorate with leftover pastry.
Bake at 350° F for 45 minutes, until pastry is golden brown in color.

Try the nut loaf or the bird gets it.

Bean There Casserole • Hodge Podge •
Home-cooked Black Beans • Honey-Roasted Carrots
• Hot to Trot Scalloped Potatoes • Izer's Epic Pota-
toes • Oven Roasted Vegetables • Reibekuchen •
Robin's Magic Mushrooms • Scalloped Tomatoes
• Spicy-Fried Tofu

**Tim Gould's impression of a couch potato.
(Or is he just vegging out?)**

Bean There Casserole

About 6 servings. This is a simple recipe for turning plain green beans into a hearty side dish with
lots of flavor.

**4 cups green beans,
cut in pieces
2 Tbsp butter
1 tsp salt
½ tsp pepper
1 tsp sugar
1 Tbsp flour
1 onion, finely chopped
1 cup sour cream**

Cook green beans until almost done.
Melt butter, stir in flour, seasonings, and onion.
Add sour cream, mix well, then heat thoroughly.
Fold in the drained vegetables and place all
in a buttered pan.
Mix the butter and bread crumbs, then mix in the
cheese.
Spread over the top of the beans.
Bake at 400° F for 20 minutes.

**Topping:
2 Tbsp melted butter
¾ cup dry bread crumbs
1 cup cheddar cheese,
grated**

Variation: Carrots can be used in place of the green
beans. Cut them in rounds and cook until almost done.
Note: To reduce fat content you can use ½ cup plain
yogurt and ½ cup sour cream.

"Bean there, done that."

Veggie Side Dishes

Hodge Podge

This simple vegetable dish was always a favorite at my Aunt Shirley's. Ideally, fresh new vegetables should be used.

---

6 cups of any combination fresh vegetables such as: baby carrots, new potatoes, green or yellow beans, broccoli, snow peas, new green peas, or lima or broad beans

**¼ cup butter
1 cup milk**

Cook vegetables in boiling, salted water until tender.
Start with those requiring longer cooking, such as beans, then add peas, carrots, potatoes, and broccoli.
Drain cooked vegetables and reserve ¼ cup of the liquid.
Melt butter in warmed milk and liquid from vegetables (do not boil.)
Pour over vegetables and place in a serving bowl.
Sprinkle with parsley and pepper.

Top tip from Dr. J. Kazimirski: Add a bay leaf to the water for extra flavor. Rice Dream or soy milk with potato or rice flour can be used in place of milk.

Home Cooked Black Beans

Black beans can be used for burritos, enchiladas, in a soup, or with rice for a good hearty meal.

**1 cup dried black beans
cold water or low-fat chicken stock
1 medium onion
2 cinnamon sticks
4 cloves garlic
1 Tbsp ground cumin
⅛ tsp nutmeg (optional)
salt to taste**

Soak beans overnight in ample cold water.
Rinse well and cover in fresh water or chicken stock. Heat to boiling, then reduce heat and keep at a low boil.
Chop and add the onion, break the cinnamon sticks into 2-3 pieces (big enough to remove later) and add with the nutmeg and cumin.
Finely chop or grate the garlic, and either sauté first (for a more pungent flavor), or add it raw.
Cook at a low boil until soft, adding extra water as needed.
Remove cinnamon pieces and add salt to taste.
Serve with rice and sour cream, or use to fill burritos.

Although sometimes they can be a little rude later on, there is nothing like a bowl of home-cooked beans.

54

Honey-Fried Carrots

These are good with almost any main course.

3-4 large carrots, sliced
2 Tbsp honey
2 Tbsp butter or vegetable oil
1 Tbsp soy sauce
1/4 tsp cinnamon
sprinkle of nutmeg
1/2 tsp garam masala
(optional)

Slice carrots into large oblong pieces about 2mm thick.
Heat oil or butter in a frying pan or skillet.
Stir-fry carrots, tossing with soy suace and spices.
Serve warm when tender.

Hot-to-trot Scalloped Potatoes

This is a Swiss version of scalloped potatoes, served up crisp and delicious.

5-6 medium potatoes
1 medium onion
1½ cup milk
3 Tbsp butter
2 Tbsp flour
salt and pepper
1 cup cheddar cheese, grated

Wash, peel and thinly slice the potatoes.
Finely slice the onion.
Layer potatoes and onion in a casserole dish.
Melt the butter in a saucepan and add the flour.
Gradually add the milk and mix well to avoid lumps.
Season with salt and pepper.
Pour this mixture over the potatoes and onions.
Sprinkle with some extra black pepper and top off with grated cheese.

Bake covered at 375° F for 30 minutes.
Remove cover and bake until potatoes are tender, about 20 more minutes.

Izer's Epic Potatoes
by Martin Stenger

Try these for breakfast, or dinner, or even along with a main course ... good anytime!

5 medium-large spuds (potatoes)
¼ cup olive oil
½ cup grated sharp cheddar cheese (optional)
dash of salt and pepper

Wash potatoes, then grate on to cutting board.
Squeeze grated potatoes to drain out excess water.
Pre-heat skillet to medium-high heat with half of the oil.
Add potatoes and spread out evenly.
Cook for about 10 minutes.
Carefully scrape potato crust with a spatula (metal if possible) and remove from skillet, in one piece.
Add the rest of the oil, then flip potatoes to the other side while keeping everything intact, like a big pancake.
Add salt, pepper, and cheese on top
Cook for 10 more minutes, or until perfectly golden-brown.
Serve with salsa, ketchup, or Izer's sauce.

Izer's sauce
Mix: ¼ cup ketchup, 2 Tbsp mayonnaise, and ½ tsp Tabasco sauce.

Oven-Roasted Vegetables

These vegetables go well with any main course.

zucchini
eggplant
mushrooms
cherry tomatoes

olive oil
mixed herbs

Wash the vegetables.
Slice the zucchini in thick slices (about ½ inch).
Slice eggplant into thinner slices, and halve each.
Keep the cherry tomatoes and mushrooms whole, unless they are quite large, then slice in half.

Place zucchini and eggplant on a cooking sheet.
Sprinkle with olive oil and dried herbs ("herbs de Provence" or oregano).
Cook at 420° F until almost tender.
Add cherry tomatoes and mushrooms to the cookie sheet and cook everything until tender. (about 10 minutes)
Serve with main course.

Reibekuchen
by Christian Lemmerz

A German version of potato pancakes, served up with applesauce. Healthy and delicious. (Serves 4-5)

4-5 onions **2 lb (1 kg) potatoes** **3-4 eggs** **1 Tbsp flour** **parsley, nutmeg** **salt and pepper to taste**	Chop onion finely. Peel potatoes and rinse to remove excess starch. Grate potatoes, mix with the eggs, flour, and seasonings, and let them sit for 15 minutes. Heat some oil in a pan. When it's hot, put 3-inch portions of the mixture into the pan and cook on each side until golden brown.
2 lb (1 kg) apples **sugar to taste**	Peel the apples and cook them slowly (350° for an hour). Pulverize them, sweeten with a little sugar if needed. Serve with the potato pancakes.

Robin's Magic Mushrooms
by Robin Gould

These tasty mushrooms are great with almost any main course.

1 small onion **10-15 mushrooms** **3 Tbsp butter** **3 Tbsp dry white wine** **or cooking sherry**	Slice the onion finely. Slice the mushrooms into fairly thick pieces. Melt the butter in a frying pan and add the mushrooms and onions. Fry until they start to brown, then add the white wine and toss well. Serve warm.

Use regular mushrooms for this — they are much easier to swallow than the atomic variety!

Scalloped Tomatoes

An interesting casserole that makes a great side dish.

1 cup diced celery	Sauté celery and onions in butter until just tender.
½ cup finely chopped onion	Blend in flour.
2 Tbsp butter	Butter toast and cut in ½-inch cubes.
2 Tbsp flour	
1 large can tomatoes (about 3½ cups)	In a large casserole dish, combine the onion and celery mixture with the tomatoes, half the toast cubes, sugar, and seasonings.
3 slices bread, toasted	
1 Tbsp sugar	Bake at 350° F for 30 minutes.
1 tsp salt, pepper to taste	
2 tsp prepared mustard (regular or 1 tsp Dijon)	Top casserole with remaining toast cubes and cook for another 20 minutes.

Spicy-fried Tofu

This spicy tofu recipe gives tofu lots of character. It can be eaten on its own with rice, or added to many other dishes.

1 package firm tofu	Cut the tofu into mid-sized, flat pieces, or cubes.
2-3 Tbsp vegetable or olive oil	Heat the oil, then add the tofu.
½ tsp sesame oil (if available)	Fry on one side first, until golden brown, sprinkling on the spices as it cooks.
2 tsp ground cumin	Turn the tofu over, then toss it around in the pan until it is well covered in spice. Cook well.
1 tsp garam masala (optional) (recipe page 9)	When almost done, add the soy sauce and let it absorb or fry off, while still tossing.
½-1 tsp chili powder	
1 Tbsp soy sauce	

Note: The same method can be used to fry soft tofu when it is used in place of hamburger-type meat. Instead of cutting the tofu, crumble it into the pan and stir well when frying. It may need to cook longer as there is usually more moisture in soft tofu.

Pasta & Pizzas

Pasta & Pizzas

Introduction

Needless to say, the variety of meals that fall under the heading of "pasta" can (and does) take up whole recipe books. Pasta is the easiest and most enjoyable way to load up on those much needed carbs before and after a race. The pasta recipes that follow range from very quick and simple to some that are a bit more involved, but well worth the effort.

In my travels to races around the world, I have found that aside from Italy, where pasta is a true delicacy, most restaurant versions are not nearly as good or healthy as homemade. Often, in the name of "gourmet cooking," an excess of oil, cream, and cheese is used.

For the more adventurous cooks, I have included several homemade pasta noodle recipes. Otherwise, most of the dishes are quick and simple to prepare and ideal for the cyclist in a hurry. *Bon appetite!*

Oodles of Noodles

This section outlines some of the pasta noodle options available. There are many different kinds and shapes of pasta, but the list is too exhaustive to attempt to outline here! For quick reference, we've illustrated most of the noodles used in this book on page 62.

Pasta is usually made from eggs and flour. There are many variations on that base. Quinoa, spelt, and rice, for example, can be used by people who are allergic to wheat. "Durum semolina" is the flour derivative usually used to make pasta noodles, though plain or whole wheat flour also can be used.

The quickest cooking pasta is fresh, since it has not been fully dried out. It takes only minutes to cook and is noticeably more flavorful than most dried noodles. Even store-bought fresh pasta tastes great, and is worth the extra pennies.

Still, dried noodles have some advantages of their own. Although they take longer to cook, they absorb more liquid, and expand to almost double the bulk. That makes them the better choice if you are planning to pack some groceries for "on the road" cooking. Dried pasta is sometimes made with whole wheat flour, or alternative grains, whereas fresh store-bought pasta is almost exclusively made from durum semolina. Don't be fooled by those nice, green spinach noodles; they are still made with white flour!

Making your own noodles at home is not too difficult and could even be done while on the road. A pasta maker has two rollers which squeeze the pasta dough, thus smoothing it out, to the right thickness. The same effect can be achieved by using a rolling pin to roll it out nice and thin. A pasta maker also has a cutting attachment which creates the thin strips of fettuccine or spaghetti noodles. When making homemade noodles without a pasta maker, it is easiest to make lasagna or ravioli noodles, since they don't need to be cut. I've included a couple of basic pasta recipes for anyone who wants to give it a try.

See the pasta trail guide on page 62 for an outline of most of the pasta noodles used in these recipes.

Spinach, tomatoes, and herbs are added to pasta dough to create color and extra flavor.

If you are looking for whole wheat pasta, you will probably have to buy the dried variety.

Quality, fresh noodles are available in many grocery stores.

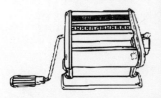

If you can get your hands on a pasta maker, go for it!

If you want to try making your own pasta before investing in a pasta maker, lasagna, gnocchi, or ravioli can all be made without one.

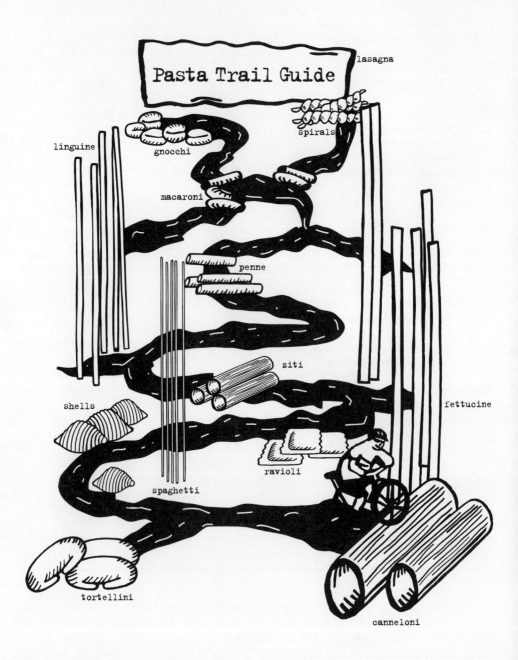

Basic Pasta

2 large eggs
1½ cups unbleached white
or durum semolina flour
water or vegetable oil,
as needed

Pasta maker method:
Starting with the widest
setting on the machine,
put a portion of the pasta
dough through 6-8 times,
folding in half each time.

Sprinkle with flour as
needed to keep the dough
from sticking. Thin the dough
by putting it through
gradually narrower settings.
This dough can then be used
for lasagna, or placed
through a cutter to make
various thin noodles such as
linguine, fettuccine, or
spaghetti.

Place the flour on a clean surface and make a
deep well in the center. Put the eggs (slightly beat-
en) in the center, then begin to stir them in with the
flour. Keep mixing until you can begin to knead
the dough with your hands. If it is still too crumbly
or dry, sprinkle a little water or oil until it is the
right consistency (pliable but not sticky). After
kneading for a few minutes, cover and let sit for
an hour.

Manual method (for lasagna):
Place a portion of the dough on a lightly floured
surface and roll out to about twice its size. Fold in
half and repeat this 6-8 times. Roll out thin, and
cut as desired. For lasagna, cut into rectangles.
Dry for an hour and cook in boiling, salted water.

Pasta can also be frozen for future use. It should be
dried for an hour or so, then tossed in extra flour
before freezing.

Note: See next page for ravioli directions.

Whole Wheat Spinach Pasta

½ cup cooked, drained
spinach (see note)
2 large eggs, beaten
1½ cups whole wheat
pastry flour
½ cup durum semolina or
fine white flour
1 Tbsp olive oil
white flour as needed

If you have a blender, put the spinach in a blender
with the eggs and blend. If not, mix manually.
Mix the flours together on a smooth surface.
Make a well in the center and add the spinach
and egg mixture and oil. Knead for 5-10 minutes
to make an elastic, but not sticky dough. If it is
still sticky add more white flour (spinach adds a
lot of extra moisture).

After kneading, cover and let sit for an hour.
You are now ready to put it through the pasta
machine or roll out as above.

Note: Fresh spinach should be puréed. Frozen spinach is the
easiest to work with. It doesn't usually require blending, but
should be heated well to get rid of excess moisture. Canned
spinach may also be used but needs to be well drained.

Gnocchi

Gnocchi is made with potato as well as flour. It goes especially well with a simple tomato sauce.

---

3 medium potatoes, boiled
2 cups flour
1 egg (optional)
additional flour as needed

Serve with sauce of choice

Note: I usually mix the boiled gnocchi with tomato sauce, cover with grated cheese, then bake to melt the cheese and keep it warm. This makes things easier when you are having guests.

Uncooked gnocchi does not keep well in the fridge. (Use that as your excuse for eating it all!)

Boil the potatoes until tender (about 20 minutes).

Drain and shake off excess water.

Mash the potatoes and keep them warm, in the pot.

Place flour on a surface and make a deep well in the middle. Add mashed potatoes, stir in the egg, and mix well with the flour. Knead on a floured surface, adding extra flour as needed.

The dough will be much softer than regular pasta dough, but shouldn't be too sticky. Break off small pieces of dough at a time and roll with your hand to about pencil thickness. Cut these into 1-inch pieces and curl into the gnocchi shape by gently pressing one end with your index finger and pulling it toward you (they should curl up into ovalized blobs). Sprinkle these with some flour to keep them from sticking. Dry for an hour or so, tossing occasionally so they don't start to stick to the surface.

Cook in lots of lightly salted water.

Spinach & Ricotta Ravioli

This is a popular classic that can be a bit "fiddly" to make, but well worth the effort

---

½ cup cooked, canned or frozen spinach, well drained
½ cup ricotta cheese
¼ cup finely grated parmesan cheese
black pepper to taste
1 egg
1 Tbsp flour

Note: If the filling seems too soft, the likely culprit is excess water from the spinach. You can correct this by adding some bread crumbs to the mixture.

Make basic pasta or spinach pasta (see page 63).

Mix the filling ingredients together in a bowl, and season with salt. If using a ravioli maker, place a little of the mixture in at a time, and let dry for an hour before cutting and separating.

To make this manually, roll out prepared dough nice and thin like you would for basic pasta. Cut into 2-inch circles with a cookie cutter. Place about 1 Tbsp of the filling in the center of each ravioli shell and fold over. Seal with a little water to make the edges stick. Dust with flour and leave to dry for an hour.

Cook in plenty of boiling salted water, for 3-5 minutes.

You've got half the meal chosen. What now?

Basic Steps

(1) Wash and peel any vegetables to be added. Slice or chop into appropriate sizes.

(2) Sauté the garlic and/or vegetables. When making a tomato based pasta, add the tomato sauce and simmer before serving.

(3) Serve over top of freshly cooked pasta. Add extra black pepper, salt, fresh herbs and parmesan as desired.

Pasta Sauces

Pasta sauces, though of infinite variety, are usually made from one of three bases: oil/butter, cream, or tomato. You can start with the simplest form, then add veggies or cooked meat of choice to create a different effect each time.

Often a simple topping, like butter and garlic sauce, is just right on its own, and you can always have your vegetables as a salad, or a steamed side dish. Straying from the basic sauces is a matter of picking some of your favorite ingredients and trying them out together. No matter which type of sauce is used, the dish always tastes better when topped off with freshly grated parmesan cheese and freshly ground black pepper.

Compared with store-bought preparations, homemade pasta sauces usually turn out much better. Almost every good sauce follows just a few basic steps, most of which can be done while the water is boiling to cook the pasta! If you are unable to find fresh basil, most store-bought Pesto is not a bad alternative, but otherwise, stick with homemade!

Pasta is best when served immediately after cooking, unless it is tossed with some kind of sauce to prevent it from becoming sticky. When having guests over for dinner, it is easier to make a pasta dish that can be left in the oven to cook or be kept warm until it is time to eat.

Butter and oil sauces are the quickest to prepare.

The oil or butter provides a rich flavor and is irresistible when used to fry garlic. Uncooked oil such as flax seed goes well tossed with pasta, when parmesan, salt, and pepper are added.

Cream sauces usually start with an oil or butter base and have cream or condensed milk added. Parmesan cheese is often used to thicken this sauce. A low-fat alternative that works well is 2-percent evaporated milk. It seems to provide a rich flavor without all the added fat found in cream.

Tomato Sauces

The best tomato sauce is prepared from garden-grown or healthy store-bought tomatoes. But who has time to do that anymore?!

All of the tomato-based sauce recipes in this book start with fresh or plain canned tomatoes. The list below refers to the various pure tomato preparations used in the recipes to follow.

Of course, you can also buy a variety of spaghetti sauces with spices, vegetables, or meat already added. These work okay if you are really pressed for time, but they're never as good as homemade!

Canned tomatoes can be used whole, chopped, crushed, or puréed.

• **Canned whole tomatoes** These are best in casseroles, stews, and dishes where the extra liquid can be absorbed, or where you want the consistency to be more like a soup. Tomato paste can always be added when a thicker sauce is desired.

Chopped tomatoes can be used for casseroles, baked dishes, curries, or soups.

• **Chopped tomatoes** Like whole tomatoes, these often have extra liquid. Best used for less-rich tomato sauces such as needed for cabbage rolls. Tomato paste can be added to make thicker as usually required for pasta sauces.

You can make tomato sauce from fresh tomatoes by boiling, peeling, and crushing them, and then removing the seeds.

• **Tomato sauce** This tomato preparation is very smooth but often quite liquid. It can be used as the basis for pasta sauce with tomato paste added to thicken. It can also be used to thin out tomato paste to use for pizzas. Good for some soups, casseroles, and curry dishes.

Creamed tomatoes (U.K.): This British version of crushed tomatoes is available in a convenient "longlife" container, where unused portions can be stored.

• **Crushed tomatoes** Crushed tomatoes are usually about the right consistency for most pasta sauces, being thick and rich. I use these often. If crushed tomatoes are being used for pizza sauce, sometimes extra tomato paste is still required to prevent a soggy crust.

Tomato purée (U.K.): This is the British version of tomato paste, but comes in a handy resealable jar, or even a toothpaste-like tube!

• **Tomato paste** This is a concentrated form of tomatoes, which can be used to thicken any tomato sauce preparation. It is the best consistency for pizza sauce, either on its own or thinned out with some tomato sauce.

Alfredo Sauce • Butter Garlic Sauce • Butter Veggie Sauce • Judy's Fresh Herb Sauce • Lentil Tomato Sauce • Prima-Veggie Sauce • Retro Sauce • Sautéed Veggie Sauce • Sensational Pesto Sauce • Spaghetti Sauce • Sun-dried Tomato Sauce

Hey thar young fellar, don't gimme no sauce!

Luke Mellor, future World Cup racer at his first Grundig race, Plymouth, England 1995.

Pasta Sauces

Alfredo Sauce

This well-known cream-based sauce can be made lighter and tastier than the restaurant version — right in your own kitchen!

**3 Tbsp butter
½ tsp salt
pepper to taste
¾ - 1cup 2% evaporated
milk or cream
½ cup parmesan
cheese, grated**

Melt the butter in a frying pan and sauté any vegetables you want to include.

Add the milk and season with salt and pepper.

Thicken it up with grated parmesan cheese and serve over fresh, hot pasta.

Vegetables of choice such as red and green peppers, snow peas (mange-tout), broccoli, sliced carrots, peas, cherry tomatoes, or mushrooms

Notes: I use low-fat evaporated milk to give it a rich-tasting flavor without the added calories, but this recipe also works just fine with plain milk or cream. As with the other sauces, many combinations of sautéed vegetables work well with this.

67

Butter Garlic Sauce

This sauce goes well with both plain pasta and cheese-filled ravioli or tortellini.

3-4 cloves of garlic, finely chopped (more if desired!)
4 Tbsp butter
pepper to taste
parmesan cheese, grated

Heat butter in a frying pan and sauté garlic until golden brown.

Toss with cooked pasta and serve with lots of grated parmesan cheese.

Note: Keep in mind that the amount of butter can easily be reduced. I normally start cooking with two tablespoons, then add more after the garlic (or veggies) have been cooked.

Butter Veggie Sauce

This is one of my favorites with the crisp vegetables making a nice contrast to the pasta.

¼ cup butter
½ cup snow-peas (mange-tout)
2 carrots, thinly sliced
½ each red and green pepper
10-12 cherry tomatoes
3-4 cloves of garlic, chopped
pepper to taste
parmesan cheese, grated

Heat butter in a frying pan and briefly sauté carrots, mange-tout and peppers.
Add garlic and cook until veggies are slightly tender.
Add cherry tomatoes last and heat thoroughly.

Toss with cooked pasta and serve with plenty of grated parmesan cheese.

Note: This can also be made using olive oil. The amount of oil or butter can be reduced.

Judy's Fresh Herb Pasta Sauce
by Dr. J. Kazimirski

This simple sauce is totally awesome! Make with as many fresh herbs as you can gather.

pasta noodles of choice
(fresh is best)
¼ -½ cup olive oil
6-10 fresh ripe Roma
tomatoes
3-5 cloves garlic, minced,
crushed, or grated
2 cups fresh basil

All or any of the following
fresh herbs:
oregano
tarragon
sage
chives
parsley

Cook the pasta noodles.
Prepare the sauce using about ¼ cup olive oil per two servings of pasta.

Gather the fresh herbs together and chop finely. (Either use an herb mill or roll a bunch of the herbs into a tight ball and hold together while chopping.)

Chop the tomatoes and prepare the garlic.
Mix all the ingredients together in a bowl then toss with cooked pasta.
Top it off with fresh grated parmesan.

Variation: This same sauce can be tossed with boiled or baked baby potatoes. Top it off with coarse (sea) salt.

Lentil Tomato Sauce

This is a substantial sauce that turns pasta into a full protein meal.

1 cup lentils, cooked

2 Tbsp olive oil
3 cloves garlic, minced
1 onion, finely chopped
1-2 cups vegetables of choice
½ cup cooked spinach
1 large can tomatoes,
crushed or chopped
2 Tbsp tomato paste

2 tsp cumin powder
1 tsp chili powder
salt and pepper to taste
1 tsp garam masala
(optional, recipe page 9)

Rinse and cook the lentils, starting with cold water. Boil until the lentils are soft, adding extra water when needed. (They'll cook more quickly if pre-soaked!)

Heat oil in a large frying pan and cook the garlic and onions.
Add vegetables of your choice.
Stir in the tomatoes, spinach, lentils, and tomato paste.
Thicken as needed with extra tomato paste.
Season with spices, salt, and pepper.
Simmer until the vegetables are tender.

Serve over fresh, cooked pasta.

Variation: Use a can of chick-peas instead of lentils.

Prima-Veggie Sauce

This is my favorite, with broccoli, carrots, and zucchini.

¼ cup butter or olive oil
1 cup broccoli, washed and stems peeled
½ each, red and green pepper
1 medium zucchini, quartered and sliced into thick pieces
1 carrot, thinly sliced in ovals
3-4 cloves of garlic, finely cut
salt and pepper to taste
parmesan cheese, grated

Heat some of the butter or oil in a frying pan, and sauté broccoli until tender-crisp.

Add carrots and zucchini and stir-fry for 2 minutes.

Add peppers, garlic, salt, and pepper and cook for another 5 minutes.
Add the remaining oil.

Either toss with cooked pasta, or serve on top. Sprinkle with lots of grated parmesan cheese.

Retro Sauce

This sauce is the homemade version of popular prepared spaghetti sauces.

1 onion, chopped
3-4 cloves garlic, minced
2 Tbsp vegetable oil
1 can crushed or chopped tomatoes
tomato paste as needed
½ tsp salt, pepper to taste
1 tsp sugar (optional)
2 tsp oregano

Sauté onion and garlic in vegetable oil.

Add canned tomatoes and seasonings, and thicken with tomato paste as desired.

Simmer for 10-15 minutes and serve on top of pasta along with parmesan cheese.

Note: If you prefer it more savory, leave out the sugar. (It makes it taste more like store-bought!)

A classic spaghetti sauce

Sautéed Veggie Sauce

3 Tbsp olive oil	Heat oil in a large pan.
1 medium eggplant	Chop the eggplant into small cubes and add to
3 cloves garlic, minced	the hot oil.
1 zucchini, sliced	Toss well until tender. Add the garlic and onion
1 green pepper, sliced	and fry for a minute before adding the zucchini
1 onion, chopped	and red pepper.
1 large can crushed or	Finally, stir in the tomatoes and thicken if needed
chopped tomatoes	with tomato paste.
tomato paste as needed	Season with salt, pepper, and oregano, then sim-
salt and pepper	mer for 15 minutes.
2 tsp oregano	Serve over cooked pasta.

Sensational Pesto Sauce

This is one of the easiest and most flavorful sauces you can make. Awesome dudes!

1 bunch fresh basil,	If you have a blender or food processor, combine
stems removed	all the ingredients together, aside from the grated
rinsed and patted dry	parmesan, and blend.
2 cloves garlic	Without a blender, you need to finely chop the
(or more — but they're	basil, crush the garlic and pine nuts, then mix well.
***much* stronger raw)**	
1 Tbsp lemon juice	Cook pasta and toss in the pesto sauce until well-
3 Tbsp olive oil	covered. Sprinkle with plenty of parmesan cheese,
½ cup pine nuts	black pepper and additional pine nuts.
black pepper	
Freshly grated	**Note:** When using the manual method, you might want
Parmesan cheese	to use more oil in place of crushed pinenuts as a labor-saving device.

Spaghetti Sauce

This is similar to basic spaghetti sauce (Retro Sauce), but more substantial with tofu and extra vegetables added.

1 package tofu
½ tsp cumin powder
2 Tbsp olive oil
3 cloves garlic, minced
1 large onion, finely chopped
2 celery stalks, chopped fine
1 zucchini and ½ cup broccoli, cut into medium pieces
1 carrot, sliced
½ cup sliced mushrooms
1 large can tomatoes, crushed or chopped
1 can tomato paste
1 tsp oregano, chili powder
salt and pepper to taste

In a frying pan, cook tofu by frying in oil and spices.
Add more oil if necessary and sauté garlic, onion, celery, and mushrooms.
In a large pot, heat another Tbsp of oil and add broccoli first, then zucchini, and carrot.
After 5 minutes, add the tofu mixture, canned tomatoes, and spices.
Bring to a boil, simmer over low heat for ½ hour.
Add tomato paste to thicken, as needed.
Serve on top of cooked pasta.

Note: Instead of, or in addition to tofu, you can add chick-peas or cooked green lentils. These make it an even more substantial sauce.

Sun-dried Tomato Sauce

This tasty sauce is more oil-based since sun-dried tomatoes, unlike the fresh or canned variety, are often stored in oil.

3 Tbsp olive oil
1 cup thinly sliced carrots
4 cloves of garlic, finely diced
10 mushrooms, sliced
1 medium zucchini, quartered and sliced into thick pieces
5-6 sun-dried tomatoes, cut into pieces
½ green pepper
salt and pepper to taste
¼ cup pine nuts
parmesan cheese, grated
2-3 Tbsp sun-dried tomato or olive oil (optional)

Prepare vegetables.
Heat oil in a frying pan and sauté carrots until tender-crisp.
Add garlic, mushrooms, zucchini, and green pepper and toss while cooking.
Mix in sun-dried tomatoes, pine nuts, and extra olive oil (if needed).

Season with salt, pepper, and oregano.

Put on top of cooked pasta and serve with grated parmesan cheese.

Lentil and Vegetable Lasagna • Izer's Lasagna • Leek and Tuna Pasta Bake • Low-Fat Fettuccine Alfredo • Macaroni and Cheese • Penne Arrabiatta • Simple Greek Pasta • Spaghetti Carbonara • Spinach Canneloni • Spinach and Ricotta Lasagna • Sun-dried Tomato and Cream Cheese Lasagna • Basic Pizza Dough • Basic Pizza Sauce • Chévre Pizza • Greek Style Pizza • Pesto Pizza • Spinach and Ricotta Pizza • Veggie Pizza

Pasta Dishes & Pizzas

Lentil & Veggie Lasagna

lasagna noodles
(see "basic pasta" on page 63)
1 cup cooked green lentils
2 Tbsp olive oil
1 pack medium-firm tofu (optional)
1 Tbsp oregano
4 cloves garlic, minced
1 onion, finely chopped
¾ cup broccoli, chopped
¾ cup zucchini, chopped
1 can tomato paste
2 cans crushed tomatoes
1 cup low-fat cottage cheese
1 cup grated mozzarella

This lasagna is not as rich as some others, but when you add lentils (or tofu) it becomes a very filling meal.

If using dry noodles, cook until almost soft.
Cook the lentils until soft (1-1½ hours).
In a large frying pan, heat the oil and fry the broccoli. Add the zucchini, onion, and garlic.
Add one tin of tomatoes, half the tomato paste, and spices.
Cook gently for 15 minutes.
Mix the rest of the tomatoes and paste with the lentils. If using tofu, add it to the lentil mixture.

In a deep, oven-proof dish, spread a layer of vegetables, and cover with a layer of lasagna, cottage cheese, and then a layer of the lentils.
Continue alternating layers, ending with the tomato sauce. Cover with mozzarella cheese.
Bake at 400° F for about 40 minutes.

Izer's Lasagna
by Martin Stenger

This lasagna by Martin is "different every time" and always good!

1 zucchini
1 yellow squash
salt and pepper
olive oil
1 medium sweet potato
12-16 oz lasagna noodles
2-3 cloves garlic
2-4 cups tomato sauce
1-2 cups parmesan, romano, or asiago cheese (fresh grated)
1 medium eggplant
10 large mushrooms, thinly sliced
2 cups fresh washed spinach, with stems removed (optional)
5 Roma tomatoes, thinly sliced

Slice eggplant, zucchini, and yellow squash into ⅛-inch slices, place on cookie sheet, and sprinkle with oil and salt.
Bake sweet potato whole for 30 minutes at 350° F, then slice thinly.
Place with veggies on cookie sheet and cook for another 15-20 minutes.

Pre-cook lasagna noodles to *al dente* texture (almost cooked, but slightly chewy).
Crush garlic and fry in olive oil before adding to tomato sauce. Season with salt and pepper to taste.

Cook spinach and drain excess water.

Assemble layers in lasagna pan:
Start with noodles dipped into sauce or spoon sauce over noodles, followed by veggies and cheese.
Don't make vegetable layer more than ½-inch thick.
Place Roma tomato slices on top with the last of the sauce around the sides.
Top with the remaining cheese and cook in oven at 375° F for 45 minutes.

Note: If you are using fresh or homemade lasagna noodles, they will cook easily while the lasagna is in the oven and require no pre-cooking. When using dry noodles, it is best to pre-cook them. You can add them uncooked, as long as they are covered by extra tomato sauce and the lasagna is cooked at 350° F for *at least* 1 hour.

Following tradition, Nick has been racing for 17 years, starting when he was in the "school boy" category. He is experienced on the road, track, and in cyclo-cross, as well as being one of Great Britain's top mountain bike racers. He earned a silver medal at the 1995 British Nationals to add to his long list of achievements. His other sports and interests include pubs, music, and "DIY" projects (carpentry).

Thanks to Sarah for help with the recipes.

Nick Craig
Birchvale, England

Favorite foods: Sticky toffee pudding and custard, tuna bake, pasta and sauce
Pre-race evening meal: Pasta with meat, water
Pre-race breakfast: Muesli, toast and jam, tea
Race drinks and food: Maxim plus blackcurrant flavor
Vitamin supplements: Vitamin C and multi-vitamin

Pro·file

Leek and Tuna Pasta Bake
by Nick and Sara Craig

This is a simple and healthy, high-protein dish that makes a good main course meal.

Ingredients	Directions
2 Tbsp (1 oz) butter	Melt butter and add chopped leeks
1 large leek	with milk and cream.
2 Tbsp cream	Cook on low heat until leeks are soft.
1 cup milk	Add yogurt, tuna, and sweet corn.
1 cup plain, low fat yogurt	Add French mustard, and salt to taste.
1 large tin albacore tuna, (packed in water)	Cook pasta until almost done.
1 tin of sweet corn	Place pasta in the bottom of an oven-proof dish
1 Tbsp French mustard	and cover with the tuna, leek, and corn sauce.
salt to taste	Sprinkle cheese over the top , followed by ground
pasta shells	black pepper.
grated cheese	
ground pepper	Bake for 10-15 minutes at 350-375° F.

Low-Fat Fettuccini Alfredo
by Chrissy Redden

Chrissy says, "It's one of my favorite pasta dishes."

fettuccini noodles (fresh is best!)	Cook fettuccini, drain, and return to pot.
1 cup cottage cheese (2%)	Meanwhile in a blender, blend cottage cheese until smooth.
¼ cup parmesan cheese	
1 egg	Add parmesan cheese, egg, and spices, then blend until smooth.
¼ tsp nutmeg	
3 slices bacon, chopped	Pour into saucepan with cooked pasta and heat, stirring constantly.
¼ tsp pepper	
chopped basil or parsley	Add bacon and any variations if desired.

Variations: Chopped cooked ham, 1 can salmon, 1 can tuna, 1 cup frozen peas (cooked), ½ cup kernel corn, 1 cup cooked mushrooms, cooked broccoli, etc...!

Macaroni and Cheese

This is an all-time favorite, so either make extra or serve with a large salad or side dish.

2 cups cooked macaroni	Cook macaroni in boiling, salted water.
White sauce:	Start white sauce by melting the butter in a small pan and lightly sautéing the onion.
1 Tbsp butter	
1 onion, finely chopped	Add flour to make a paste, then gradually add the milk, mixing well to avoid lumps.
1 Tbsp flour	
½ tsp salt	Remove from heat, and stir in the cheese.
1 cup milk	Season with salt and pepper to taste.
black pepper	
1 cup cheddar cheese, grated	Drain the macaroni and place in a casserole dish. Stir in the cheese sauce, and cover with bread crumbs.
1 cup bread crumbs	

Bake at 350° F for 30-45 minutes.

Alex is a well-known road racer with countless victories throughout his 15-year career. He is often remembered for being the first North American to wear the yellow jersey in the Tour de France. He is now "retired" from racing and works for Soft Ride Suspension, but has reportedly been spotted on bike rides and at races as well! His other interests include downhill, cross-country (skate-style), and telemark skiing, as well as ice hockey.

Alex Stieda
Bellingham, WA

Favorite foods: Pasta (with cream sauces!), oatmeal, roast beef, and penne arrabiata
Pre-race evening meal: High-complex carbo with chicken or fish
Pre-race breakfast: Oatmeal with fruit and toast
Race drinks and food: Water
Vitamin supplements: Vitamin C

Pro·file

Penne Arrabiata
by Alex Stieda

This pasta is nice and hot, but if you prefer it mild, adjust the amount of chili pepper. A super tasty meal.

extra virgin olive oil
2-3 cloves garlic, crushed
approximately ½ cup
sun-dried tomatoes in olive oil
chili pepper flakes

1 large can whole Italian plum tomatoes
basil, oregano
salt and pepper

penne pasta
(must be an Italian brand!)

Heat 1-2 Tbsp oil with garlic. Brown but don't burn. Add thinly sliced sun-dried tomatoes and sauté.
For a spicy sauce, add chili pepper flakes to oil and garlic.
Pour in can of plum tomatoes including the juice, and break down tomatoes while cooking. Turn down to simmer. Add basil, oregano, salt, and pepper to taste.
Simmer for as long as possible — preferably an hour. Cook penne noodles *al dente*. Serve sauce over noodles with some fresh basil and grated cheese.

Variations: Add peas to simmering sauce, or pour sauce over some grilled chicken pieces and sauté.
Top tip by Dr. J. Kazimirski: Try sambal olek (Thai-style chili pepper sauce) in place of chili peppers.

Pedal Pasta

A rich and tasty deep dish pasta.

1 cups pasta noodles,
either spirals or ziti-type tubes
1 large eggplant
2-3 Tbsp olive oil
3-4 cloves garlic
1 small onion
1½ cups crushed tomatoes
1 tsp oregano
salt and pepper to taste
½ cup low fat cottage cheese
½ cup ricotta cheese
½ cup mozzarella cheese,
grated

Cook the pasta until "al dente" texture.
Cube the eggplant into small-sized pieces.
Heat the olive oil and fry the garlic and onion for a minute.
Add the diced eggplant and toss while cooking until almost tender.
Add the tomato sauce and season with salt, pepper, and oregano.
Place the pasta noodles in a large, deep oven-proof pan and mix well with the tomato sauce mixture.
Stir in the ricotta and cottage cheeses.
Cover with grated mozzarella cheese.
Bake at 350° F for 30 minutes.

Note: You may also use all ricotta or all cottage cheese instead of a mixture of the two.

Ravioli Bake

This is a good way to make a package of ravioli go further (at least an extra mile).

1 package ravioli (or even better- homemade)
1 cup chopped broccoli
1 cup chopped zucchini
¾ cup cauliflower florets
1 small to medium sized onion
3-4 cloves minced garlic
1 large can chopped or crushed tomatoes
1 can tomato paste
salt, pepper, oregano
1 cup cheddar cheese
¾ cup breadcrumbs

In a large frying pan or pot heat some oil and add the broccoli pieces, stirring frequently.
After a minute, add the cauliflower.
Keep stirring, and add a little more oil and the onion and the garlic.
Toss in the zucchini pieces and finally add the tomatoes and tomato paste.
Season with salt, pepper, and oregano.
Reduce heat and simmer until broccoli is tender-crisp.
Cook the ravioli in lots of lightly salty water. Toss with the vegetable mixture and place in an oven-proof dish. Cover with grated cheddar cheese and breadcrumbs if desired. (oh yeah...)
Bake at 350°f for 20-30 minutes. Enjoy!

Alison has been racing for 11 years (already!) and is a multiple world mountain bike champion (1994, 1995 and 1996). Among her many other achievements are a silver medal at the 1996 Olympics in Atlanta, and a bronze medal in the 1991 road worlds. Her other sports and interests include playing ice-hockey, baking, and drinking coffee (she can often be found frequenting the many cafes of North Vancouver).

North Vancouver, British Columbia

Alison Sydor

Pro·file

Pre-race evening meal: Salad, pasta, chicken, and a small dessert

Pre-race breakfast: Oatmeal or pancakes (my own mix from home "Capers")

Race drinks and food: Endura and Optimizer

Vitamin supplements: Multi-vitamins when travelling only

Nutritional hints: "If you're too busy or lazy (like me) to prepare or eat your fruits and veggies, buy a juicer."

Simple Greek Pasta
by Alison Sydor

Great for cooking while on the road — quite easy and very tasty. Serves four (or three cyclists).

1 lb fusilli or rotini pasta
1 Tbsp olive oil
1 Tbsp minced garlic
4 large tomatoes, chopped
⅓ cup black olives, chopped (optional)
½ cup crumbled feta cheese
½ cup chopped, fresh parsley
2 Tbsp chopped fresh basil
¼ cup freshly grated parmesan cheese

Cook pasta noodles in boiling, salted water. Meanwhile, heat oil in a large skillet over medium heat. Stir in garlic.
Add tomatoes and cook for three minutes, stirring. Transfer to pot with drained pasta and add: olives, feta, parsley, and basil.
Toss to mix.
Sprinkle parmesan on each serving.

Mediocrates: the simple Greek

Spaghetti Carbonara
by Mike and Emily Kloser

Serves about 4 (or 2 if Mike is eating with you!).

1 lb spaghetti	Cook spaghetti until *al dente*.
2 tsp olive oil	Meanwhile, heat oil in a pan over medium heat.
4 cloves garlic, minced	Add garlic and cook until golden, 2-3 minutes.
3 oz fat-trimmed ham	Discard half of the garlic. Add ham for 1-2 min-
¼ cup white wine	utes, then pour in wine and simmer for 1 minute.
1 egg	Remove from heat.
2 egg whites	In a bowl, whisk egg, egg whites, cheese, and
½ cup parmesan cheese, grated	parsley. Add pepper.
	Drain pasta and return to pot.
¼ cup fresh parsley, chopped	Working quickly, add egg and cheese mixture plus ham mixture, then toss.
	The heat from the noodles will cook the eggs.
salt and pepper	Serve with salt and pepper at the table.

Spinach and Ricotta or Feta Cannelloni
by Nick and Sarah Craig

An awesome pasta dish — so make lots because everyone will be asking for seconds!

1 small onion, chopped	Sauté onion, garlic, parsley, and herbs briefly.
3 cloves of garlic, crushed	Add tomatoes and wine and simmer for 15 min-
2 Tbsp parsley	utes or until onions are soft.
basil or mixed herbs	Place the tomato sauce in the bottom of a casse-
fresh or tinned tomatoes	role dish.
6 Tbsp white wine	Mix spinach and ricotta or feta in a bowl with
ricotta or feta cheese	half of the butter (⅛ cup) and marjoram.
6 oz chopped spinach	Fill the pasta tubes with the spinach and cheese
¼ tsp marjoram	filling and place on top of tomato sauce.
pasta-strips or rolls (cannelloni)	Melt remaining butter and mix in flour and milk to make a sauce. Add cheese, salt, and pepper.
2 oz (¼ cup) butter	Pour this cheese sauce over cannelloni and sprin-
2 cups milk	kle with parmesan.
1 Tbsp flour	Bake at 350° F for 25 minutes.
grated (cheddar) cheese	
ground pepper and salt	

Spinach and Ricotta Lasagna

This lasagna is a bit rich with all the cheese, but very good. You can reduce fat content by using low-fat cottage cheese.

lasagna noodles
(recipe page 63)
1 Tbsp oil
1 onion, finely chopped
2 cloves garlic, minced
1 large can crushed tomatoes
tomato paste
1 tsp salt
1 tsp basil (optional)
2 tsp oregano
1 cup spinach
(frozen or fresh cooked)
¾ cup ricotta cheese
1 cup grated mozzarella
¼ cup grated parmesan

Cook noodles to *al dente* if using packaged pasta (no need to pre-cook if using fresh noodles).
Sauté onion and garlic lightly in oil.
Add tomatoes and seasoning and leave to simmer.
Thicken with tomato paste as needed.
Mix together the ricotta cheese and spinach.

In a large, deep dish spread a layer of the tomato sauce over the bottom and cover with a layer of lasagna noodles, then a layer of the ricotta and spinach.
Continue alternating layers, ending with the tomato sauce. Sprinkle the mozzarella cheese over top and finish off with parmesan.

Bake at 400° F for 20-30 minutes.

Sun-dried Tomato and Cream Cheese Lasagna

The sun dried tomato mixture is rich and distinctly flavored, but not overpowering when mixed with these extra veggies.

lasagna noodles
(recipe page 63)
2 Tbsp olive oil
½ cup chopped broccoli
2 small carrots, sliced
1 zucchini, chopped
tomato sauce, tomato paste
½ cup spinach,
cooked or frozen
¼ to ½ cup sun-dried
tomatoes, puréed
½ cup chick-peas, puréed
¼ cup cream cheese
oregano, black pepper
1 cup mozzarella, grated
parmesan cheese

Cook noodles to *al dente* if using packaged.
Heat oil and cook vegetables in a frying pan.
Add some tomato sauce and simmer until slightly tender.
Prepare spinach and add 2 Tbsp tomato sauce, and 1 Tbsp tomato paste.
Purée softened sun-dried tomatoes in a blender, then purée chick-peas.
Blend well with cream cheese.
Thin with a little tomato sauce to make mixture spreadable.
In a casserole or lasagna dish, layer as follows: tomato sauce, noodles, vegetable mixture, noodles, spinach, noodles, sun-dried tomato mixture, noodles. Spread tomato sauce over top, sprinkle with oregano and pepper, and cover with cheeses.

Bake at 350° F for 20-30 minutes.

Basic Pizza Dough

This is the basic recipe along with some cooking tips.

½ cup warm water
1 tsp sugar
1 Tbsp (1 package) dry yeast

1 cup warm water
1 Tbsp oil
1 tsp sugar

½ tsp salt
3 cups flour

Whole wheat flour can be used instead of white or unbleached flour. To keep the dough pliable, I usually use half of each type.

Remember to let the dough rise again before adding toppings.

Place water, yeast, and sugar in a small bowl and let sit for 10 minutes.
Combine additional water, sugar, and salt in a medium-sized bowl, then add yeast mixture.
Mix in flour, a little at a time, and knead for 10 minutes. If dough is sticky, add more flour as required.
Place dough in a lightly oiled bowl, cover, and let rise until almost double (45 minutes).

After the dough has risen, take ⅓ (thin crust) to ½ (thick crust) of the dough per pizza and roll out on a floured surface into a circular shape.
If you like your pizza crust to be on the thick side, then use more dough per pizza.

After rolling out, place on a greased pizza pan and spread to cover the edges.

Let rise for another 10-15 minutes.
Add toppings and bake at 425° F for 15-20 minutes. Check to see that the bottom of the crust is browned before removing from oven.

Notes: A thick crust should be pre-cooked for 10 minutes before covering with toppings to ensure it cooks through. If pre-cooking, the crust should be pricked all over with a fork.

If a thin crust is preferred, keep in mind the dough does rise a bit more once it's been spread onto the pan, so you can make it quite thin to start with, as it will still expand.

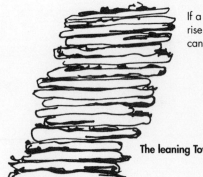

The leaning Tower of Pizza

Basic Pizza Sauce

2 Tbsp olive oil
½ onion, finely chopped
2-3 cloves garlic,
grated or finely diced
1 cup creamed
(or crushed) tomatoes
tomato paste as needed

This sauce can be used to top off all kinds of pizzas. This makes more than enough to cover two pizzas.

Heat oil in a frying pan and add onion and garlic. Sauté for a minute and add creamed tomatoes. If creamed or thick stewed tomatoes are unavailable, start with tomato paste and thin out with water or tomato sauce to make a fairly thick sauce.

Spread pizza sauce on prepared crust.

Note: When using toppings that have a high water content, such as tomato slices or spinach, it is best to make a thicker sauce.

It is best to coordinate your clothing to match your evening meal. For pizza sauce a red sports coat is a perfect choice.

Greek-Style Pizza
by Bill Hurley

pizza dough
(recipe opposite page)

Topping:
1 large onion
4-6 cloves of garlic
2 Tbsp olive oil
1 (14oz) can tomato paste
1 can artichoke hearts
1 cup feta cheese
1 can pitted black olives

Other toppings can be added such as green and red pepper, tomato slices, zucchini slices, or pre-cooked broccoli.

This recipe yields two pizzas, but ingredients can be halved to make just one.

Make pizza dough as per recipe.

While dough rises, prepare toppings.
In a frying pan, sauté the onions and garlic in oil. Add tomato paste and simmer for 5 minutes (if too thick, add some water or tomato sauce).

Once dough has risen, roll out and fit into two pizza pans, pressing into place. Spread tomato sauce mixture evenly over top and cover with sliced olives and artichoke hearts. Top off with feta cheese.

Bake at 350° F for 20-25 minutes, until crust is golden brown.

"Crumbling Parthenon" provides classic flavor.

Pro·file

Penny is a U.S. national downhill champion. She also does television commentary at the World Cups, and can often be seen "harassing" tired cross-country racers at the end of their race! Penny's other sports and interests include skiing, reading, motorcycles, driving fast (downhiller instincts?), and her nephews and nieces.

Penny Davidson
Big Bear Lake, California

Favorite foods: Baked yams, homemade pizza, fresh fruit, pasta, pancakes
Pre-race evening meal: Pasta, green salad, and maybe some cookies
Pre-race breakfast: Oatmeal, toast, juice, banana
Race drinks and food: PowerBar, Endura Pro Optimizer
Vitamin supplements: Metagenics
Nutrition hints: "I stay away from lots of dairy and like simple flavors. Try to eat fresh foods of good quality."

Penny's Pizza
by Penny Davidson

Penny for your thoughts: "Balance your diet with all food types. Don't be excessive; use moderate amounts and variety."

10-12 garlic cloves
about ½ cup olive oil
basic pizza dough
(recipe page 82)
4-8 oz shredded mozzarella
4-8 oz crumbled goat's
milk cheese (chévre)
12 sun-dried tomatoes,
reconstituted and slivered
¼ cup minced fresh parsley
salt
freshly ground black pepper
¼ cup freshly grated
parmesan cheese

To roast the garlic, preheat oven to 300° F.

Place the garlic cloves in a small baking dish and toss with 3 Tbsp of the olive oil. Cover the dish and bake until tender but not browned (about 30 minutes). Remove from the oven, chop and reserve for later. Prepare the dough and preheat the oven to 425° F.

Shape the pizza dough and brush all over with olive oil. Top with mozzarella and chévre, leaving a ½-inch border around the edges. Sprinkle with the reserved garlic, tomatoes, parsley, salt, and pepper. Drizzle evenly with olive oil. Transfer to oven and bake for 15-20 minutes, until bottom of crust is golden brown.

Remove from oven and sprinkle with parmesan cheese. Slice and serve immediately.

Mike has been racing for 12 years or so, and is well known as one of the first American pro mountain bikers to compete in Europe. He is very consistent in World Cup races and is competitive in the NORBA series. He has competed in downhill skiing in the past, and it remains an interest, as is golfing. "Family time" is another interest of Mike's with the arrival of family additions Heidi and Christian. Special thanks to Emily for help with the recipes!

Vail, Colorado

Mike Kloser

Favorite foods: Mexican, Italian, pesto pizza, barbeques, and fresh salads
Pre-race evening meal: Pasta
Pre-race breakfast: Cereal and toast
Race drinks and food: Carbohydrate drink
Vitamin supplements: Multi-vitamin
Nutritional hints: "Eat healthy, minimize fats, eat your pre-race meal at least two hours prior to racing."

Pro·file

Pesto Pizza
by Mike and Emily Kloser

Pesto pizza has the very distinct flavor of fresh basil, garlic, and sun-dried tomatoes. Enjoy!

pizza dough (recipe page 82)

Prepare pizza dough.

1½ cups basil leaves
¼ cup parmesan cheese
¼ cup fresh lemon juice
¼ cup pine nuts
1 Tbsp olive oil
1-3 garlic cloves, crushed

Put sun-dried tomatoes in boiled water to hydrate. Combine basil, parmesan, lemon juice, pine nuts, olive oil, and garlic cloves in a blender and blend until puréed.

¾ cup sun-dried tomatoes
1 cup sliced mushrooms
feta cheese
scallions, chopped
mozzarella cheese

Preheat oven to 425° F.
Oil pizza pan.
Spread dough on sheet and poke holes in it with a fork. Put in oven for 8-10 minutes.

Meanwhile, sauté mushrooms in water or olive oil. Take crust out and spread pesto over it.
Scatter toppings and cheese on top and put back in oven for a few minutes until cheese melts.

Spinach and Ricotta Pizza

Here's that irresistible combination of spinach and ricotta cheese again.

**1 portion pizza dough
(recipe page 82)**

Prepare pizza dough as per recipe.

**Pizza sauce:
1 Tbsp olive oil
½ small onion
2 cloves garlic
¾ cup creamed tomatoes**

Heat oil in a frying pan and add onion and garlic.
Sauté briefly and add creamed tomatoes.
Spread pizza sauce on prepared (unbaked) crust.

Place spinach evenly on pizza, a piece at a time.
Gently spread ricotta cheese onto spinach leaves.
Cover with sliced tomatoes and mozzarella cheese.

**Toppings:
½ cup cooked,
drained spinach
ricotta cheese
mozzarella cheese
thinly sliced tomatoes
(optional)**

Bake at 425° F for 15-20 minutes.

Veggie Pizza

This simple combination of toppings makes a healthy and filling pizza.

**2 portions pizza dough
(recipe page 82)
pizza sauce
(recipe page 83)**

Prepare pizza dough and pizza sauce as per recipes.

Heat oil in a pan and begin to cook broccoli and eggplant. Add a little water to lightly steam.

**Toppings:
3 Tbsp olive oil
1 cup broccoli
½ eggplant
thinly sliced (optional)
1 zucchini, finely sliced
1 cup sliced mushrooms
1 red pepper, finely sliced
2 tsp oregano
1 cup mozzarella cheese
parmesan cheese**

Remove from heat when almost cooked. Spread pizza dough on pans and after 10 minutes, cover with sauce.

Place cooked veggies on first, followed by raw mushrooms, red pepper, then zucchini slices. Sprinkle with oregano.

Top with mozzarella and parmesan cheeses.
Bake at 425° F for 15-20 minutes, until bottom of crust is golden brown.

photo by Robert Oliver

Baked Goods

Introduction

The smell of home baking has to be one of the most appetizing aromas in the world. Whether you have bread, muffins, or pies in the oven, the smell of fresh-baked goods is sure to fire up your appetite, and remind you that baking is worth the time and energy spent.

This chapter covers how to make homemade bread and pastry that any novice or sports-class baker can master. Along with baked goods, there is also a sweets section that involves the use of two commonly abused "banned" substances — sugar and fat. Be sure to indulge in moderation, or you may test positive for excess weight gain!

Impress your friends and family with real homemade bread!

Whole Wheat Bread (recipe)

I usually make the "double" version of this recipe, which yields 4 loaves of bread. The dough is more difficult to work with though, so if you are new to bread making it is better to try this smaller amount first.

Ingredients (for two loaves):

½ cup warm water
1 tsp honey or sugar
1 Tbsp dry yeast

1¾ cup warm water
1 Tbsp sugar or honey
1 Tbsp molasses
2 tsp salt
2 Tbsp oil

3½ cups whole wheat flour
2-2¼ cups white flour

Summary of steps:

1) prepare yeast
2) mix liquids
3) add flour
4) knead
5) let rise
6) shape into loaves
7) let rise
8) bake
9) enjoy!

How to Make Bread

Most people think of making bread as time-consuming, and too difficult to attempt. Although it does take a bit of patience waiting for the dough to rise, the actual time spent working isn't long. The main skill to master is that of "kneading," or working the dough into a smooth and elastic consistency. As with most things, this is best learned by doing, and is even easier when you have someone to show you how the first time. My husband, Tim, learned his baking techniques from his mom just a few years ago, and now bakes awesome bread.

Preparing dry yeast

When using regular dry yeast, it first needs to be mixed in ½ cup of warm (but not hot) water with 1 tsp of sugar. While this is growing (for 10 minutes), you can measure out the rest of the ingredients.

Mixing

Combine the remaining ingredients, except the flour, in a large bowl. Add the yeast mixture. Gradually add the flour, first stirring with a spoon and then by hand. When the dough is no longer wet, remove from the bowl on to a well-floured surface.

Kneading

Kneading usually takes about 10 minutes, but should be continued if the dough is still sticking to your fingers or to the kneading surface. The dough is worked by pressing it down hard with the heels of your hands, turning it 90 degrees, bringing it back toward you, then pressing down again. You continue these motions, adding more flour as needed until the dough becomes noticeably smoother and no longer sticks to the surface. Form the bread into a ball, and place it in a lightly greased bowl. Cover with a damp cloth and find a nice, warm place to let it rise. Leave for one hour, or until it nearly doubles in size.

Last Steps

"Punch" or press the risen dough down, and divide it into even portions. Roll and shape each portion into a loaf. Place in greased loaf pans, cover with a damp cloth, and let rise again for about 20 minutes. Bake in a pre-heated oven at 375° F for 40-45 minutes. When nicely browned, remove from oven. Leave in the loaf tins for 5 minutes, then take out to cool on a wire rack.

These recipes make enough for either 1 double-crust pie or 2 single-crust pies. Leftover dough can be stored in the freezer.

Basic Pastry
1½ cups unbleached flour
½ cup vegetable shortening
½ tsp salt
¼ cup cold water

Whole Wheat Pastry
1½ cups whole wheat pastry flour
½ tsp salt
½ cup butter, cut into pieces, or shortening
¼ cup water plus more as needed

Baking guidelines:

1 Crust, Baked:
Place dough in pie plate. Prick with a fork in several places, and bake at 400° F until lightly browned (15-20 minutes).

Unbaked 1- or 2-crust:
Place dough in pie plate and add filling. Cover with the rolled-out pie shell (if 2 crust) and cut 3 slits in the top. Bake according to recipe.

Homemade Pastry (pie crust)

Pastry is used for a number of meals and desserts. For a more nutritious pastry, whole wheat flour is best. Because of the extra grains and fibre in whole wheat flour, it can be more difficult to work with, and sometimes causes a tough or crumbly crust. It helps to use whole wheat "cake and pastry" flour, which is milled finer than the ordinary or stone-ground variety. While the best basic pastry dough is homemade, other types, such as filo pastry, are usually better store-bought. Filo can be found in the freezer section of most grocery stores and is used for spinach pie or apple strudel. Store-bought "puff" pastry is also good, though you can make this type at home as well (recipe page 113).

Technique:

Mix the flour and salt together in a bowl. Add shortening and with two dull knives or a pastry knife, cut the shortening into the flour until it becomes fine lumps. Sprinkle the water onto the mixture, a little at a time, mixing it in with a fork or your fingertips. If the dough seems dry, sprinkle with a little more cold water. Form it into a ball and wrap in plastic. Chill for 1 hour before rolling it out.

When rolling out pastry dough, try not to handle it too much, so it doesn't get tough. Roll away from your body using light strokes and turn the pastry to keep it circular. A rolling pin is best, but I've used empty bottles before, when necessary!

Place the pie plate upside down to measure, making sure there is an extra inch of dough all the way around the pie tin. Cut off any obvious excess dough, and then gently lift the pie crust into the center of the pan. Once it is evenly in the pan, trim to the edge of the pie plate. This task can be made easier by rolling out the dough on waxed paper, which prevents the dough from sticking to the surface and helps in lifting it.

If it is a 2-crust pie, roll out the second piece a little smaller than the first. Place it on top of the pie filling and press the edges together. Trim any excess dough, and cut slits in the top to allow air to escape while the pie bakes.

Bake Sale

Banana Nut Bread • Basic Bread • Berry and
Lemon Muffins • Bran Cake • Bran Muffins •
Brown Soda Bread • Carrot-Pineapple Muffins •
Cinnamon Rolls • Corn Bread • Foccacia Bread •
Granary Bread • Griddle Scones • Hearty Corn
Bread • Health-Nut Bread

Basic Bread

You can use this basic recipe to make cinnamon
buns, bread, or even bagels

½ cup warm water
1 tsp sugar
1 Tbsp (1 package) dry yeast

Place water, yeast, and sugar in a small bowl and
let sit for 10 minutes
Combine water, sugar, and salt in a medium-sized
bowl and add yeast mixture.
Mix in flour, a little at a time, and knead for 10

1 cup warm water
1 Tbsp oil
1 tsp sugar or honey

minutes. If dough is sticky, add more flour, as
required. Place dough in a lightly oiled bowl,
cover, and let rise until almost double (about 45
minutes).

¹/₂ tsp salt
3 cups flour

After it has risen, halve the dough and form into
two loaves. Place in lightly greased loaf tins and
let rise for another 20 minutes.
Bake at 350° F for 45 minutes, or until golden
brown in color.

Note: Alternatively, you can use half (or all) of the dough
to make cinnamon rolls (page 96).

91

Pro·file

Chrissy is one of the top racers on the Canadian mountain bike scene, with seven years experience. She was overall winner of the Canada Cup series in 1994 and 1995, third at the 1994 and 1995 Canadian National Championships. Her other interests include cross-country skiing and road racing.

Chrissy Redden

Milton, Ontario

Favorite foods: Beef, chocolate, fresh baked bread, scalloped potatoes
Pre-race evening meal: Pasta and red sauce with beef and veggies
Pre-race breakfast: Oatmeal
Race drinks and food: Excel energy drink and water
Vitamin supplements: Low dose multi-vitamins
Nutritional hints: "Eat a well-balanced diet, stay healthy."

Banana Nut Bread
by Chrissy Redden

Rather than throwing out those old bananas, you can freeze them or, even better, turn them into this yummie snack!

1¼ cups flour
2 tsp baking powder
½ tsp salt
¼ tsp baking soda

⅔ cup sugar
⅓ cup margarine
1 egg
1 cup mashed ripe bananas (about three)

1 Tbsp lemon juice
½ cup chopped walnuts

In a bowl mix flour, baking powder, salt, and soda.
Cream sugar and margarine together, then add egg, mixing thoroughly.
Add dry ingredients alternately with banana and lemon juice.
Blend well after each addition.
Stir in walnuts.
Place in a greased 8½ x 4½-inch loaf pan.
Bake at 350° F for about 1 hour.
Remove from pan immediately and cool on rack.

Notes: Softened butter can be used in place of margarine. To check if the loaf is done, insert a small knife or skewer. If it comes out clean, the loaf is done.

Sara has been racing for 11 years now and is very well known on the mountain bike circuit. Among her many achievements was the World Cup series victory in 1991, unofficial world champion titles in 1988 and 1989, and a bronze medal at the 1994 World Championships. Her other sports and interests include alpine mountaineering, rock climbing, and Nordic skiing.

Sara Ballantyne
Breckenridge, Colorado

Pro·file

Favorite foods: Ethnic foods, spicy food and black bean burritos!!
Pre-race evening meal: Pasta and chicken or burritos
Pre-race breakfast: Oatmeal or couscous
Race drinks: Endura Allsport and Optimizer
Nutritional hints: "I'm a firm believer that if you have a well-rounded diet and are genetically lucky to have no serious health problems, there is no need for supplements."

Berry and Lemon Muffins
by Sara Ballantyne

These muffins make a nice snack in between meals or for breakfast with some fruit and yogurt.

1 ¼ cup all-purpose flour
¾ cup whole wheat flour
⅓ cup sugar
⅓ cup brown sugar
1 tsp baking powder
1 tsp baking soda
½ tsp salt
8 oz container lemon yogurt
¼ cup unsalted butter (melted and cooled)
1 egg, lightly beaten
1-2 tsp grated lemon peel (zest)
1 tsp vanilla
2 cups fresh or thawed, drained frozen berries

Preheat oven to 400° F. Grease 12 muffin cups.

In a large bowl, stir together flour, sugars, baking powder, salt, lemon peel, and vanilla until blended.
Make a well in the center of the dry ingredients; add yogurt and butter mixture, and stir, just to combine all ingredients.
Fold in the berries.
Spoon batter into prepared muffin cups.
Bake for 20-25 minutes.
Remove from oven and place muffin tin on a wire rack to cool for 5 minutes.
Remove from cups and finish cooling on rack.
Store in airtight container.

These muffins freeze well.

Bran Cake
by Gary Foord

In the event you ever need to "get things moving," as in after a long flight, bran is always a good choice with lots of natural fiber.

1 cup bran
1 cup sugar
1 cup raisins
1 cup flour
1 cup milk

Mix the dry ingredients first, then add the milk. Place in a square tin and bake at 350° F for 40 minutes.
Check with a toothpick until it comes out clean.

Alternatives: In place of raisins, you can use chopped, dried figs, dried apricots, or other dried fruit of your choice.

Bran Muffins
by Nancy Smith

Another healthy bran-filled treat. Use with caution, these could turn deadly if you eat too many!

1 cup flour
(preferably whole wheat)

1 tsp baking soda
1½ cups bran
½ cup raisins
1 egg, well beaten
¾ cup milk
½ cup molasses
2 Tbsp soft butter

Mix together dry ingredients and raisins.
Mix wet ingredients together and add to dry ingredients, stirring just until mixed.

Place, one large spoonful at a time, into well-greased muffin tins.
Bake at 400° F for about 15 minutes.
Check biggest muffin with a toothpick until it comes out clean.
Serve warm.

Note: These muffins taste great and make a well-balanced breakfast with some cheddar cheese on top. They can also be served with yogurt and fruit salad.

Brown Soda Bread
by Laurie Brandt

Soda bread is a quick way to make bread without having to wait for the dough to rise, since it is made without yeast.

---

2 cups whole wheat flour
2 cups white flour
½ tsp salt
1 tsp baking soda
2 cups (1 pint) buttermilk
2 Tbsp oil or butter

Mix all of the ingredients together in order.
Knead until smooth.
Form into a ball and place on greased and floured cookie sheet.
Slightly flatten the ball and score with a knife (make an "X" pattern).

Bake at 350° F for 45 minutes.

Carrot-Pineapple Muffins

I use this base recipe and substitute various fruits in place of the pineapple (such as cranberries, blueberries, or apple).

1½ cup flour
1 cup sugar (can be reduced)
1 tsp baking powder
1 tsp baking soda
1 tsp cinnamon (optional)

½ cup oil
2 eggs
1 cup grated carrot
½ cup pineapple (or fruit of choice)

Mix dry ingredients together in a large bowl.

Mix the wet ingredients together (oil, eggs, and grated carrot).
Combine with the dry ingredients, then fold in your fruit of choice.

Place in well-greased muffin tins.
Bake at 325° F for 25-30 minutes.
Check biggest muffin with a toothpick until it comes out clean.

Cinnamon Rolls

I usually make the basic bread dough, and use half of it for pizza or bread and the other half for these cinnamon buns.

½ portion basic bread dough
(see recipe page 89)

¼ cup butter, melted
½ cup brown sugar
2 Tbsp cinnamon
1 apple, peeled and grated
½ cup chopped walnuts or
pecan pieces (optional)

Make basic bread dough as per recipe.
After it has risen, take half the dough and roll out to about ¼-inch thick on a floured surface.
Mix the butter and sugar and spread on dough.
Sprinkle the apple on evenly, and top with cinnamon and walnuts.
Roll up and seal the edges. Slice into approximately 1-inch thick sections or rolls, then place in an oblong or square pan, with the sections or rolls just touching each other.
Let rise for about 15 minutes.
Bake in preheated oven at 375° F for 20-25 minutes.

They should still be moist because of the apple, but cooked through and golden brown.

Note for women only: Research has shown that the smell that arouses men most is that of cinnamon buns baking. Beware of sudden attention (especially from mechanics and bike racers who are food-obsessed anyway) while baking these buns!

Corn Bread

This is one of my all-time favorites. Goes well with baked beans, black bean soup, and stews.

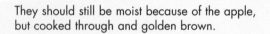

1¾ cup cornmeal
1 cup flour
1 Tbsp baking powder
¼ cup sugar

½ tsp salt

2 eggs
¾ cup melted butter
1¼ cups milk

Preheat oven to 350° F and grease an 8-inch square baking pan.

Combine dry ingredients in a large bowl.

Beat eggs and combine wet ingredients.
Stir wet ingredients into dry and mix well.
Spread mixture evenly into pan and bake at 350° F for 30-40 minutes.
Check center with a toothpick to see if it is done.
Serve warm and spread with butter.

Christian is a talented young rider who has been racing for eight years. He races downhill on the World Cup circuit and is an excellent technical and trials rider. Christian placed eighth in the 1995 World Championship in Kirchzarten. His other interests include trials and windsurfing. Being part Italian and part German, his recipes reflect his lineage.

Rheinbreitbach, Germany

Christian Lemmerz

Favorite foods: Hot Mexican or my mother's Italian cuisine, pizza and lasagna
Pre-race evening meal: Pasta or rice
Pre-race breakfast: Muesli with soy milk, bread with honey or marmalade
Race drinks and food: Water for long races, one PowerBar
Vitamin supplements: none

Focaccia Bread
by Christian Lemmerz

This classic Italian bread is excellent with spaghetti or minestrone soup, or just by itself.

3⅓ cup (1 lb) flour 1 packet (1 Tbsp) instant yeast 1 cup warm water	Mix flour, yeast, and water (see note below). Knead dough until soft. Let dough rise until it has almost doubled in size. Preheat oven to 425° F. Oil a deep pizza pan. Spread the dough on the pan (use a rolling pin).
1-1½ cup cream 3-4 eggs 1½ cup (300 g) cheese, grated nutmeg	Mix the cream, eggs and nutmeg, then the cheese. Put this mixture on the top of dough. Bake for 20-30 minutes at 425° F.

Note: If you are using ordinary dry yeast, follow the instructions on the packet (start the yeast on its own in water with some sugar for 10 minutes).
Variations: Focaccia Bread can also be topped with simple toppings such as olive oil, garlic, sun-dried tomatoes, black olives, or with herbs (oregano, basil).

Granary Bread
by Tim Gould

This is the bread we live on whenever we aren't on the road. Tim bakes it once a week, and it keeps well in the freezer.

Full Recipe (4 loaves):

5 cups white flour (1½ lbs)
4½ cups granary flour (1½ lbs)
1¼ cups bran (4 oz)
2 Tbsp yeast (1½ oz)
2 tsp salt
6 Tbsp shortening (2 oz)
4 cups warm water (1¾ pint)
1 large Tbsp black treacle (molasses)

1/2 Recipe (2 loaves):

2½ cups white flour
2¼ cups granary flour
¾ cup bran
1 Tbsp (¾ oz) yeast
1 tsp salt
3 Tbsp shortening
2 cup warm water
1 Tbsp molasses

Put flour in a large bowl and rub in shortening. Make a deep well in the center of the flour and sprinkle salt around the edges.
Crumble yeast into the middle.
Mix black treacle with warm water and pour into the center of the flour.
Wait until yeast bubbles up, then mix well with a spoon.
Remove dough from the bowl and proceed to knead on a well-floured surface.
Add additional flour as needed.
Put kneaded dough back in the bowl, cover with a damp cloth, and place in a warm area to rise for 1 hour.
Knead briefly again and shape into loaves.

Put in bread tins, cover and let rise for another 20 minutes.

Preheat oven to 425° F.
Bake at: 425° F for 20 minutes.
then at 375° F for 15 minutes.

Remove from pan and bake out of tins for 5 more minutes (unless already well-browned).

Notes: This recipe uses "live" or wet yeast, which is available at the local bakeries in England. You can use dry yeast by following the dry yeast directions for any bread. "Granary" flour is an ingredient I've never come across in North America; However, it may well be found in some health food stores. It is a type of white flour with grains added that makes especially good bread.

Jill and Tim living on bread

Griddle Scones
by Mrs. Violet

These savory scones are another contribution from our neighbor Mrs.Violet. In true Scottish tradition, she kindly brings us samples of her great home cooking.

2 cups (8 oz) flour
1 Tbsp baking powder
⅛ cup (1 oz) margarine or lard
milk or sour milk (1 tsp vinegar per cup of milk)

Place the dry ingredients in a bowl and work in the lard or margarine.
Add enough milk or sour milk to make a thick mixture for rolling out.
Lightly flour a surface and roll out the dough into two circles about ¼-inch thick each.
Cut each into quarters.
Place in a large, lightly greased skillet or frying pan and cook one side at a time.
Test for doneness by touching the sides of the scones. They are done when the sides are no longer sticky when touched.

"Health-Nut" Bread

This bread is similar to plain whole-wheat bread, only much heavier without the white flour. The dough isn't as smooth, but the bread is a meal in itself!

½ cup warm water
1 tsp honey
1Tbsp dry yeast

1¾ cup warm water
1 Tbsp honey
2 Tbsp molasses
½ cup sunflower seeds
½ cup walnuts
2 tsp salt
2 Tbsp oil

½ cup oatmeal (optional)
5½-6½ cups whole wheat flour (or part white)

Place yeast, sugar, and water in a small bowl and let sit for 10 minutes.
Combine the remaining ingredients in a large bowl (except the flour and oatmeal).
When ready, add the yeast mixture.
Stir in 3 cups of flour and let rise for 10 minutes.
Add remaining flour and knead for 10-15 minutes.
Add flour as needed, so dough isn't sticky.
Form into a ball, place in the bowl, cover, and let rise for 1 hour or until about double in size.
Punch down dough and form into loaves.
Place in greased loaf pans and let rise again for 20 minutes.
Bake at 375° F for 40-50 minutes. Remove from oven, and after 5 minutes place loaves on wire rack.

Susan won the bronze medal at the first Olympic mountain bike race in 1996. She also won a silver medal at the 1994 World Championships and has numerous top World Cup placings to her credit. She has been racing for 11 years and is just getting better every year! Her other sports and interests include cross-country ski touring, snowshoeing, trail running, and reading.

Susan DeMattei
Gunnison, Colorado

Favorite foods: Anything from Italy (cheese and olive oil — yum!), brownies, and Mexican dishes
Pre-race evening meal: Pasta with pesto sauce, bread, and salad
Pre-race breakfast: Pancakes and coffee (1 cup)
Race drinks: Water, coke, and/or Exceed
Supplements: An occasional multi-vitamin
Nutritional hints: "Try to get your daily intake of vitamins and minerals (and calories) from FOOD! (That's what it's intended for.)"

Hearty Corn Bread with Cheese and Sun-dried Tomatoes
by Susan DeMattei

The name of this says enough!

½ cup sun-dried tomatoes
1½ cups cornmeal
½ tsp baking soda
4 Tbsp butter, melted
3 large eggs
1 17oz can creamed corn
2 cloves garlic, minced
1 onion, finely chopped
1 cup (6 oz) mozzarella cheese, grated
2 Tbsp minced basil leaves
1 cup sour cream (non-fat if desired)

Pre-heat oven to 375° F.
Pour some hot water over the sun-dried tomatoes and let sit until softened (about 5 minutes).
Combine cornmeal and baking soda and mix well.
Stir in butter, eggs, corn, garlic, onion, mozzarella, basil, and pepper. Mix well.
Drain tomatoes and chop coarsely.
Stir tomatoes into batter, then add sour cream.
Heat an oiled cast-iron skillet or large casserole over high heat, or in oven, until sizzling.
Pour in batter.
Bake for 50-60 minutes until golden and fairly firm, but not hard.
Serves 6-8 people.

Almond Slice • Appelebread • Apple Crisp • Chocolate Fridge Cake • Chocolate-Chocolate Chippers • Custard Pie • Date Squares • Fruit Crisp • Fat-and Sugar-Free Cake • Fruit Crisp • Gingersnaps • Gingerbread Cake • Health-Nut Cookies • Holiday Ring Cake • Homemade Rice Pudding • Moist Apple Pud • Mom's Apple Pie • Mom's Pumpkin Pie • Nova Scotian Strawberry Shortcake • Olde English Porter Cake • Puff Pastry • Rhubarb Bread Pudding • Rhubarb Cream Pie • Rollover Pavlova • Rocky Choc-Chocs • Sex in a Pan • Simple Sponge Cake • Sticky Toffee Pudding • Tim's Ultra-Delicious Lemon Cheesecake • Tropical Fruit Salad

Chinese take-out, Beijing style!

Toute de Sweets

Almond Slice
by Mrs. Gould

A tad on the decadent side, but makes a great evening snack.

½ **portion basic pie dough (recipe page 90)**	Line a Swiss roll tin with pastry and prick all over, using a fork.
jam	Spread jam thinly over top.
½ **cup (4 oz) butter**	Cream butter and sugar, then add eggs, almond essence, and ground almonds.
¼ **cup (4 oz) castor sugar (fine white sugar)**	
1 **cup (5 oz) ground almonds**	Spread on top of jam and top off with sliced almonds.
2 **eggs**	
1 **tsp almond essence**	Bake at 350° F for 20 minutes.
2 **cup (2 oz) flaked almonds**	**Note:** I usually use strawberry jam, but any kind will work.

Pro·file

Ernst has come into the sport of mountain biking relatively late in life and has raced for eight years. As Austria's top rider, he has amazing endurance and is a good climber, making him consistently well-placed in the World Cup series. Ernst is also into cross-country skiing, ski-touring, and mountain climbing. I always enjoy cooking for Ernst when we are on the road because he's got such an appetite, there's no worry about leftovers!

Austria

Ernst Denifl

Pre-race evening meal: Pasta with tomato sauce, fish
Usual pre-race breakfast: Bread, coffee, jam, yogurt, fruit
Race drinks: Isostar or Maxim, Red Bull, cola
Vitamin supplements: Multi-vitamin, vitamin C, magnesium

Applebread
by Ernst Denifl

A traditional Austrian recipe, this makes 4 loaves so the recipe can be halved if you want to try it out first.

1½ lbs apples, peeled, cored, and sliced
1½ cup (300 g) raisins
1½ cup (300 g) dried figs, cut into small pieces
2 cups (300 g) hazelnuts, cut into small pieces
1 Tbsp cocoa
3 cups (500g) brown sugar
½ cup (⅛ l) rum

Put all the ingredients, except the flour and baking powder, into a big bowl and mix well. Cover and let sit overnight.

The next day add the flour, and baking powder (and baking soda if needed), and mix into a soft dough.

Place in greased loaf tins and bake at 175°C for 60-70 minutes.

8½ cups (1000 g) self-raising flour
or: flour plus 4 tsp baking soda
1 Tbsp baking powder

Note: I haven't had time to test out this recipe, but it sounded too good to exclude. So here it is, complete with attempted German translations!

Apple Crisp

This is my old reliable recipe for a quick and "healthy" dessert. You can substitute many other fresh fruits or fruit and berry combinations for the apples.

6-8 apples peeled
2 tsp lemon juice
¼ cup brown sugar
1 tsp cinnamon
¼ tsp nutmeg

Topping:
¼ cup whole wheat flour
1½ cups rolled oats
½ cup brown sugar
½ tsp salt
¼ -½ cup butter

Slice apples and toss with lemon, sugar, cinnamon and nutmeg in a large bowl. Omit this sugar if you are using sweet apples or pre-sweetened fruit.

Place in buttered 9- x 9-inch pan or large casserole dish.

Combine dry ingredients and cut in butter. Spread evenly over apples and bake at 350° F for 45-50 minutes, or until tender.
Serve warm with a spoonful of ice cream or plain yogurt.

Note: If you are in a rush, use canned fruit such as cherries or blueberries to reduce cooking time considerably.

Chocolate Fridge Cake
by Jonathan Holmes

This recipe is courtesy of Jon Holmes from the Matlock Cycling Club.

---

8 oz. whole wheat biscuits
(cookies)
4 oz. (½ cup) butter or
margarine
2 Tbsp golden syrup
1oz. (⅛ cup) granulated sugar
1 oz. (¼ cup) cocoa
¼-½ cup chopped nuts
⅛ cup glacé cherries
⅛-¼ cup raisins (optional)
To cover: 6-8oz. chocolate

Grease a swiss roll tin or small cookie sheet.
Crush biscuits (cookies) into crumbs.
Melt margarine, sugar, and syrup in a pan.
Add biscuits, cocoa, cherries and nuts, and stir well.
Press into greased tin with a wooden spoon.
Melt chocolate on a plate over hot water.
Pour chocolate over the base and spread evenly.
Place in the fridge to set.

Chocolate-Chocolate Chippers

Recipe by Peter Stace-Smith, product development manager, Norco Products Ltd.

1½ cup margarine or butter (soft)
1 cup brown sugar
⅔ cup white sugar
2 eggs
1 tsp vanilla

Beat the egg with butter and brown sugar.
Add the vanilla.
Sift together all dry ingredients except the chocolate chips.
Blend dry ingredients into eggs, butter, and vanilla until smooth and creamy.

2⅔ cup flour
1½ tsp baking soda
8 oz chocolate chips
⅓ cup cocoa
½ tsp salt

Next fold in chips.
Drop by the tablespoon onto ungreased cookie sheets.
Bake at 375° F for 7-10 minutes
Let cool at least one minute on cookie sheets before removing to cooling rack.

Warning: Don't leave these cookies unguarded near small children, bike racers, or mechanics; a rapid reduction in quantity may occur.

Custard Pie
by Mrs. Violet

This is one of my all-time favorite desserts, so I just had to include it. Baked custard can be (and often is in our house) eaten as a meal.

2 eggs
1 Tbsp sugar
2½ cups (1 pint) milk
ground nutmeg

Beat eggs with sugar, and stir in the milk.

Strain and pour into a prepared pastry shell.
Sprinkle with nutmeg.

1-half portion pastry crust

Bake at 375° F for 45 minutes or until set.

Variation: This can be made without the pastry (as "baked custard"). Pour into a buttered pie plate and bake as above.

Top tip by Mrs. Violet: Eggs kept at room temperature provide better results for baking. If the eggs are being beaten and need to be fluffy, heat cold eggs in a pan of warm water.

Date Squares
by Nancy Smith

Date squares are naturally very high in carbohydrates. They are a bit crumbly for training rides, but if wrapped well, make a great tasting energy bar substitute.

---

1 cup dates
1 Tbsp brown sugar
½ cup water

Put dates, water, and sugar in a pot and cook gently until soft.

Crumb mixture:
1 cup flour
½ tsp baking soda
⅛ tsp salt
1 cup butter
1 cup brown sugar
2 cups rolled oats

Mix flour, salt, and soda.
Cut in butter, then add sugar and oats.

Spread half of the crumb mixture in an 8- x8-inch pan. Cover with date filling.
Pat remaining crumb mixture on top.

Bake at 325° F for 35-40 minutes.

Fat- and Sugar-Free Cake
by Sian Roberts

It's hard to imagine a cake without fat or sugar, but here it is, and it's good too!

1½ cup sultanas or raisins, soaked in tea overnight
2 cups wholemeal flour
4 even tsp baking powder
1 generous Tbsp clear honey
2 large mashed bananas
2 free-range eggs

Put all ingredients in a bowl and mix thoroughly.

Place in a lightly greased square cake tin.

Bake covered with a small gap to let out steam for 1½ hours at 350° F (gas mark 4).

"I've never seen a cake like this before."

Pro•file

Ruthie has been racing for 13 years, both road and off-road. She is one of the top mountain bike racers in the world, with a gold medal at the 1991 World Championships, and at the Grundig World Cup series in 1992. She won the NORBA national championship series in 1996. Her other interests include cross-country skiing, hiking, reading, gardening, knitting, and foreign languages.

Ruthie Matthes
Durango, Colorado

Favorite foods: Fresh mangoes, tropical fruit, brown, rice, green chilies, rice and veggies
Pre-race evening meal: Meat or fish, rice and veggies
Pre-race breakfast: "That's a secret"
Race drinks and food: Glucose polymer, PowerBars
Vitamin supplements: Multi-vitamin, iron
Nutritional hints: "Eat foods that burn clean: organic beans, rice, veggies, natural meats, lots of Evian or Volvic water, and don't forget ice-cream or treats occasionally."

Fruit Crisp
by Ruthie Matthes

Ruthie says she has made some alterations to this recipe by "Joni." In true Ruthie fashion, it has been transformed from a somewhat decadent dessert into a highly nutritious offering!

Crumb topping:
1 cup flour (can use rye, oat, or rice flour instead of wheat)
¾ cup oats
½ cup brown sugar
¼ cup melted butter
1 tsp cinnamon

Fruit mixture:
4 cups sliced fruit (ripe fruit helps it cook faster)
1 cup water
2 Tbsp cornstarch (or arrow root powder)
1 tsp vanilla
1 cup sugar (optional — Ruthie suggests none)

Mix together the crumb topping ingredients.

Press half of it into a greased 9-inch square pan. Cover with fruit.

In a small pan, cook the sugar, water, cornstarch, and vanilla, until it is thick and clear.
Pour over fruit.

Top with remaining crumb mixture.

Bake at 350° F for 45-60 minutes.
Test to see if fruit is cooked by inserting a toothpick.

Serve warm by itself, or with an ice-cream topping.

Gingersnaps

These are good cookies to have on hand to prevent you from eating those awful store-bought ones!

1 cup shortening
¾ cup white sugar
¾ cup molasses
1 beaten egg
1½ tsp vinegar

3 cups flour
1½ tsp baking soda
1½ tsp ginger
¾ tsp salt
⅛ tsp pepper

Cream together shortening and sugar.

Add molasses, egg, and vinegar, and mix well.

Combine flour, baking soda, ginger, salt, and pepper. Mix together well to form a soft dough.
Roll out a little bit of dough fairly thinly on a lightly floured surface.
Cut with a cookie cutter (or any suitable circular object such as a glass). Repeat until all the dough is gone (or eaten).
Place on a cookie sheet and bake at 350° F for 8-10 minutes.

Note: This recipe makes *a lot* of cookies! They keep well when stored in an airtight container.

Gingerbread Cake
by Mrs. Violet

This traditional Scottish recipe has been passed down through the years, and is truly delicious.

½ cup margarine or butter
½ cup sugar
3 cups flour
1 tsp cinnamon
½ cup molasses
2 tsp ground ginger
1 tsp mixed spice (optional)
1 tsp baking soda
½ tsp salt
1¼ cup milk or sour milk
(for sour milk add 1 tsp vinegar)

Beat butter and sugar to a cream.
Sieve the flour (optional).
Add the salt, soda, and spices to the flour.
Stir in the treacle amongst the sugar.
Add the flour mixture and mix well.
Add the milk, a little at a time, until the batter is a rather stiff consistency.
Place in a greased 8-inch square pan and bake at 375° F for about 45 minutes.
To check for doneness insert a toothpick, which should come back clean.
Serve warm with a scoop of whipped cream.

Note: This recipe is from a notebook Mrs. Violet's sister kept (in the 1930's), when she worked as a cook. I've kept most of this recipe's original text, but had to alter some things (it didn't mention adding milk at all!).

Health-Nut Cookies

These cookies are calorie and nutrient rich, like a homemade energy bar.

½ cup brown sugar
½ cup white sugar (optional)
½ cup vegetable oil
1 beaten egg
1 tsp vanilla

½ cup mashed banana
½ cup coconut
½ cup walnuts
½ cup dried figs and/or apricots, diced
1 cup flour
½ tsp baking soda

½ tsp salt
2 cups rolled oats

Combine sugars and oil.

Add egg and vanilla.

Blend in banana, coconut, walnuts, and dried fruit.

Blend together flour, baking soda, oats, and salt.
Add to creamed mixture and mix well.

Shape into balls.
Place on cookie sheet and press lightly with a fork.
Bake at 350° F for 12-15 minutes.

Variation: Raisins or chocolate chips can be used in place of dried fruit.

Holiday Ring Cake
by Shirley Richards

This cake is nice and dense, being full of fruit and nuts. It is delicious fresh out of the oven and also freezes well.

1 cup butter or margarine
8 oz cream cheese
1½ cup sugar
1 tsp vanilla
2 Tbsp grated lemon or orange rind
4 eggs
1¾ cup flour
1½ tsp baking powder
1 cup raisins
½ cup chopped cherries
1 cup mixed fruit
½ cup chopped walnuts
¼ cup flour

Mix butter, cream cheese, sugar, vanilla, and rinds.
Add eggs one at a time, beating well after each.

Add flour mixed with baking powder.

Mix ¼ cup flour with fruit (raisins, cherries, mixed fruit, and walnuts) and add to the cake batter. Stir.

Pour into a well-greased and lightly floured cake pan or tube pan if available.

Bake in a preheated oven at 300° F for 80-90 minutes.

Home—Made Rice Pudding
by Angela Ward

This dish is a simple way to do some extra carbo-loading. Angela says she has this for P.M. races. "Yum-Yum!"

¼ cup (1½ oz) short grain "pudding" rice

2 cups (1 pint) milk

3 Tbsp (1 oz) sugar

ground nutmeg

Place rice, milk and sugar in a greased, oven-proof dish.
Sprinkle ground nutmeg on top.

Bake at 300° F (gas mark 2) for about 2 hours, depending on your preference of thickness.

For a thicker consistency, stir the "skin" on top after about an hour. Sprinkle more nutmeg on top.

Moist Apple Pud
by Sian Roberts

Keep in mind that "pud" or "pudding" means dessert in England, this is a cake rather than an American-style pudding.

1 lb apples chopped into small pieces
½ cup (4 oz) raisins
⅓ cup (1 oz) flaked almonds
¾ cup (4 oz) wholemeal self-raising flour or
¾ cup (4oz) wholemeal flour plus 1 tsp baking soda

1 Tbsp clear honey
1 free-range egg

Mix together the apples, raisins, almonds, and flour.
Melt butter and honey in a saucepan, beat in the egg, and add to dry ingredients.
Mix very well to blend evenly.

Place in a lightly greased shallow 8-inch tin and bake for 25-30 minutes at 400° F (gas mark 6).
Allow to cool slightly before cutting.
Best served with hot custard or ice cream.

"Yummie!"

Mom's Apple Pie

This classic is good anytime, anyplace, and fresh out of the oven it's even better!

1 double crust pie shell (see recipe page 90)

Prepare basic pie dough as per recipe.

**4-6 large apples
1 Tbsp butter
1 Tbsp cinnamon
¼ tsp nutmeg
½ cup sugar
3 Tbsp - ¼ cup
flour (see note)
lemon juice
(optional)**

Granny Smith

Peel apples, then cut into thin slices.
Place in a large bowl and sprinkle with spices, sugar, and flour.
Toss lightly and place in uncooked pie shell.
Top with butter and another sprinkle of cinnamon.
If the apples are fairly sweet, then add lemon juice.
Bake for 1 hour at 325° F.
Serve warm with a spoonful of vanilla ice cream, or low-fat yogurt.

Note: Add the larger amount of flour if the apples are quite juicy, like McIntosh or Spartan. Add less if they are drier like the Granny Smith variety.

Mom's Pumpkin Pie
by Nancy Smith

This is traditionally used to top off various feasts. The pumpkin makes it a more nutritious pie than some types. Then of course, you top it off with whipped cream!

**2 single-crust pie shells
(recipe page 90)
2 cans pumpkin
(about 3 cups if using
fresh)
1⅓ cup brown sugar
1½ tsp cinnamon
1 tsp ginger
½ tsp nutmeg
1 tsp salt
4 well-beaten eggs
1 cup milk
1⅓ cup evaporated milk**

Prepare pastry shells as per recipe.

Blend all ingredients until smoothly combined.

Pour into unbaked pie shells.
Sprinkle with a little extra nutmeg.
Bake at 450° F for 10 minutes, then at 350° F for 30-40 minutes.

Refrigerate, if it's to be kept more than one hour.

Makes two pies.

Note: Fresh pumpkin can be used instead of the canned variety. Fresh pumpkin needs to have the seeds removed then cooked until tender. The seeds can be roasted and eaten as a nice snack, so don't throw them away!

Tim has been racing for about 19 years now, starting off with local time trials and cyclo-cross races. He is one of the top mountain bike racers, winning a bronze medal at the 1991 World Championships, twice finishing top five in the Grundig World Cup series, and placing eighth overall in the 1995 series. His interests include baking, reading, running, collecting puncture kits, and Citroën DS's.

Tim Gould

Derbyshire, England

Favorite foods: Indian curries
Pre-race evening meal: Pasta with veggie sauce, fish
Pre-race breakfast: Oatmeal, or toast and marmite
Race drinks and food: Maxim
Vitamin supplements: None
Nutrition Hints: Guinness is good for you

Pro·file

Olde English Porter Cake
by Tim Gould

Since Porter is no longer available in England, Guinness or any dark beer is a good substitute.

1 cup butter (8 oz)
grated rind of 1 lemon
1⅓ cup soft muscovado or brown sugar (8 oz)
3 eggs, beaten
1 cup raisins (8 oz)
1 cup sultanas (8 oz)
¼ cup mixed peel (2 oz)
¼ cup glacé cherries (2 oz)
½ cup almonds (2 oz)
2½ cups plain flour (10 oz)
1 tsp cinnamon
½ tsp ground nutmeg
¼ pint Porter or Guinness

Cream the butter and sugar together in a large bowl.
Add the eggs and beat well.

Fold in the raisins, sultanas, peel, almonds, mixed spice and flour and mix.

Place in a greased deep 8-inch loaf or cake pan.

Bake at 325° F for 1 hour.
Reduce heat to 300° F and bake for 2 more hours.

Variations: As an option to the raisins and/or currants, chopped dried fruit such as figs or apricots may be used.

111

Nova Scotian Strawberry Shortcake

This strawberry shortcake uses a basic scone recipe instead of having a cake base.

___

1 batch scones, or biscuits (see recipe below)

Make scones as per recipe and cut into 6 large, circular pieces instead of smaller-sized scones.

2 pints fresh strawberries

½ cup sugar, or less if berries are extra sweet

1 cup whipping cream

Take ¾ of the strawberries and lightly mash in a bowl, adding the sugar. Slice remaining berries, saving one for the top of each dish.
Cut slightly cooled scones in half and place the bottom part in a dessert bowl.
Cover each with the mashed strawberry mixture. Place top of scone back on and cover with extra berry mixture and sliced berries.

Spoon a large dollop of whipped cream on top of each, and garnish with a whole strawberry.

Scones

You can use these for strawberry shortcake, or eat them on their own or with butter, jam, or clotted cream

___

2 cups flour
2 tsp baking powder
⅛ cup sugar
¼ cup butter or shortening

½ cup milk
1 egg

For currant scones add:
¼ cup sultanas or currants

Mix the dry ingredients in a bowl.
Cut butter into flour-baking powder mixture.
Mix egg with milk, and add to dry ingredients.
Turn onto a floured board and roll to 1-inch thickness.
Cut with a cookie cutter (circles) or into triangles with a knife.

Bake at 350° F for 10-15 minutes until golden brown.

Puff Pastry

This pastry is a little more decadent, so I usually use it with savory recipes instead of dessert pies.

1⅔ cup flour
¾ cup butter, finely diced into small cubes
½ tsp salt
½ cup iced water

Place flour and salt in a medium bowl.
Add the chilled butter cubes and, using a blunt knife or your fingertips, gradually work the butter into the flour. When the mixture has become streaky, add the iced water and mix it in. Knead the dough until the water is absorbed.

Lightly flour a surface, then roll the dough into a rectangle. Fold this rectangle in three and roll it out again. Turn it 90 degrees, fold it in three once more, and repeat the process one more time.

Cover or wrap with plastic and refrigerate for 1 hour. Remove from fridge and fold into a rectangle as before, folding in three.
Roll out to desired size on floured surface.

Rhubarb Bread Pudding
by Marjorie Soares

An excellent dessert and a good way to use left-over bread.

3 cups chopped rhubarb
1 cup sugar
3 cups (stale) bread crumbs
½ cup milk
¼ cup butter
½ cup sugar
2 eggs
1 tsp vanilla
cinnamon

In a bowl, mix chopped rhubarb with 1 cup sugar.
Place bread cubes in another bowl and pour milk over them.
In a large mixer bowl, cream butter and sugar together. Add eggs and beat well. Add vanilla.
Fold in bread mixture and then rhubarb.
Pour into buttered casserole dish and sprinkle with cinnamon.
Bake at 350° F for about 45 minutes until it is set.

Variation: As an alternative topping, you can make a streusel mixture, as for apple crisp (recipe page 103). Use a little of the topping and freeze the rest for future use.

Rhubarb Cream Pie
by Marjorie Soares

Rhubarb can be used in pies, cakes, muffins, or on its own. My aunt Marjorie's rhubarb pie is the best I've ever tasted.

2-crust pastry shell (recipe page 90) **3 cups rhubarb** **1 cup sugar** **¼ cup flour**	Prepare pastry. Cut rhubarb finely and place in unbaked 9-inch pie shell. Combine sugar, flour, and salt.
¼ tsp salt **¾ cup hot cream** **(or 2% evaporated milk)**	Blend in the hot cream and pour this mixture over the rhubarb. Cover with pastry, trim the edges, and make three slits in the top.
	Bake at 425° F for 12 minutes, then 350° F for 20 minutes or until tender.

Rollover Pavlova
by Mrs. Cynthia Gould

This dessert is truly decadent and delicious. Recommended for those in need of a lot of calories.

Meringue: **3 egg whites** **¾ cup (6 oz) castor sugar** **(fine granulated sugar)** **1 tsp corn starch** **1tsp plain or** **white wine vinegar** **additional castor sugar** **1 portion whipping cream** **fresh berries of choice** **(blueberries and strawber-** **ries work well)**	Beat egg whites. Add sugar a third at a time, while continuing to whip the meringue. Fold in corn starch and vinegar and mix well. Use a non-stick Swiss roll tin (11- x 8-inch with a raised edge), or if necessary, a small cookie sheet. Line with parchment paper or lightly grease. Spread meringue mixture evenly onto pan and bake at 350°F (gas mark 4) for 20 minutes. Tip out onto a clean dish towel, which has been lightly sprinkled with fine sugar. Leave to cool. Place on serving plate and spread with whipped cream and berries. Using the towel, gently roll up. Slice to serve, and garnish with berries.

"About the Author"

Jill started road racing 9 years ago, and made the move to off-road in 1992. The highlights of her racing career include two World Cup 3rd placings and three national champion titles. She races primarily in Great Britain now, having recently retired from the World Cup circuit. Her hobbies range from hiking, running, ice-hockey and skiing to reading, writing, music and artwork.

Jill
Derbyshire, England
Smith-Gould

Favorite foods: Indian curries, eggplant anything
Pre-race evening meal: Pasta with veggie sauce
Pre-race breakfast: Oatmeal, or toast and Marmite
Race drinks and food: High Five, Red Bull
Nutrition hint: "If you are prone to mood and energy swings, they may be caused by sudden drops in blood sugar, so it helps to avoid simple sugars and excessive caffeine.

Rocky Choc-Chocs

These decadent cookies make a great emergency energy bar — just beware of a possible sugar and chocolate overdose.

½ cup milk ½ cup butter or margarine 2 cups sugar	Place the milk, butter, and sugar in a large saucepan. Heat slowly to boiling point, cook for a minute or two. Turn off the heat, leaving it on a warm burner.
1 tsp vanilla 3 cups oatmeal 6 Tbsp cocoa 1 cup shredded, unsweetened coconut ½ cup finely chopped pecans or walnuts (optional)	Stir in oatmeal, cocoa, and vanilla. Remove from stove-top and add coconut and nuts. Mix well, then slop onto ungreased cookie sheets, one blob at a time, while the mixture is still hot. Leave to set for an hour in the refrigerator.

Sex in a Pan
by Elladee Brown

Entice your senses with this seductively delicious dessert!

Base:
1½ cups flour
½ cup butter or margarine
2 tsp ice water
½ cup almonds (ground)

8 oz cream cheese
1 large container Cool Whip®
(or whipped cream)
1 cup icing sugar
8 oz instant chocolate
pudding mix
3 cups cold milk
1 tsp vanilla

Mix base like pastry dough and roll out to fit a 13- x 9-inch pan. Prick all over with a fork. Bake for 25 minutes at 350° F, and leave to cool.

Mix the cream cheese in a bowl and cut in 1 cup Cool Whip® and the icing sugar. Spread this mixture over the cooled crust.

Mix the chocolate pudding and let stand until thickened. When thick, spread over the creamed cheese mixture, then top with remaining Cool Whip®. Sprinkle with grated chocolate and refrigerate until ready to serve.

Simple Sponge Cake
by Tim Gould

This simple cake is transformed into a wonderful dessert with the addition of fresh strawberries and cream.

Cake:
⅓ cup (3 oz) castor sugar
(fine granulated)
3 eggs
¾ cup (3oz) flour

Beat egg and sugar until light and fluffy.
Fold in flour and mix.
Place in two lightly greased 8-inch cake pans.
Bake at 350° F (gas mark 4) for 20 minutes.
Remove from the oven and cool on a wire rack.

Filling:
strawberry jam
fresh strawberries, sliced
whipped cream

When cool, spread the top of one cake with a light layer of jam, sliced berries, and some whipped cream. Place the second cake on top and spread with whipped cream and garnish with some fresh berries.

Sticky Toffee Pudding
by Sarah and Nick Craig

Beware, this traditional British dessert is a secret national treasure; very sweet and possibly addictive.

Cake:
⅓ cup (5 oz) sugar
½ cup (3 oz) butter
2 beaten eggs
1¼ cup (6 oz) self-raising flour
(or flour and 1 tsp baking powder)
1 cup (6 oz) chopped dates
¾ tsp baking soda
½ tsp vanilla essence
2 tsp coffee essence (optional)
¾ cup (6 fl oz) boiling water

Sauce: see recipe below

Cream together sugar and butter.
Add eggs and flour and stir together.
Add dates, baking soda, vanilla, coffee essence (if desired) and water.
Mix together and put into a greased pan or mold about ⅔ full.

Bake at 350° F for 30-45 minutes.

Note: Keep in mind again that though it's called "pudding," this is a cake-based dessert.

Sticky Toffee Pudding Sauce

½ cup (4 oz) butter
1 cup (6 oz) soft brown sugar
½ cup (¼ pint) double cream
(or whipping cream)
⅔ cup (2 oz) pecans

Melt the butter, brown sugar, and cream over low heat.
Add the nuts.
Turn the pudding (cake) out on a large dish and pour hot sauce over the top.

Serve immediately (sooner if possible).

Tim's Ultra-Delicious Cheesecake
by Tim Gould

If I hadn't fallen for Tim the first time I met him, the cheesecake he makes definitely would have hooked me.

Base:
7 oz chocolate chip cookies
(about 1½ cups when the cookies are crumbled)
½ cup (3½ oz) butter
a handful of raisins

For the base, crumble the cookies well (crushing them with a rolling pin works).
Melt the butter in a small pan and stir in the cookies and raisins.
Spoon this mixture into a suitable cheesecake pan and press it down to form the base.

1 large or 2 small
packages cream cheese
½ pint cream
(about 1 cup)
1 lemon
¼ cup (2 oz) castor sugar
(fine white sugar)

Cream the cheese in a bowl and stir in the sugar.
Grate in some of the lemon rind, then squeeze in the juice and mix well.
Whip the cream and fold it into the cheese mixture.
Spread this mixture on to the base after it has set.
Garnish with sliced fresh fruit or berries.
Refrigerate for at least one hour.
Tastes even better after a full day in the fridge.

Tropical Fruit Salad

This dessert has potential for being a bit rich if a lot of coconut milk is used, but this version is lighter.

2 medium bananas
½ fresh pineapple
1 small can either mango pieces or papaya
2 fresh mandarin oranges
(or 1 small can)
⅓ cup coconut milk
½ cup low fat yogurt
sliced almonds

Cut the bananas into quarters then slice into chunks.
Chop the pineapple into bite-sized pieces.
Separate the mandarin oranges into pieces.
Place the chopped fruit in a large serving bowl and add the mango, yogurt, and coconut milk.
Stir to mix.
Refrigerate until ready to serve.
Sprinkle with sliced almonds before serving.

Miscellaneous

Introduction

Despite the trivial-sounding nature of this chapter's title, it contains some seriously mouth-watering recipes. Many of the soups are quite substantial and could easily be served as main courses.

The sections on breakfast foods and quick fixes provide some further meal ideas. The recipes for sauces and most of the salads are meant to provide accompaniments to other foods.

Soups

Armenian Lentil Soup • Cream of Anything Soup • Dahl • Leek and Potato Soup • Lentil and Carrot Soup • Minestrone • Miso Soup • Mom's Lentil Soup • Mom's Black Bean Soup • Quickie Tomato Soup • Quick Vegetable Soup • Split Pea Soup • Tomato Soup • Veggiestock

As a professional cyclist one has to learn to wear many hats (not to mention a helmet).

Armenian Lentil Soup
by Stephen Bearne

This hearty soup was recommended to me by Dr. Judy Kazimirski — so it *must* be good!

1½ cup dried lentils (green)
6 cups vegetable stock
½ cup chopped dried apricots
1-2 Tbsp vegetable oil
1 cup chopped onions
2-3 cups cubed eggplant
½ cup chopped tomatoes (fresh or canned)
1 green pepper
¼ tsp each: cinnamon, allspice, cayenne
1 Tbsp paprika
1½ tsp salt
3 Tbsp fresh parsley
1 Tbsp chopped fresh mint (optional)

Rinse the lentils and bring them to a boil in the stock. Reduce heat and simmer in a covered pot for about 20 minutes.

Add the chopped apricots and simmer covered for another 20 minutes.

Meanwhile, sauté the onions in oil until translucent, then add the eggplant and ¼ cup of water. Cook on medium heat until eggplant is tender, then add everything else.

Cover and cook for 10 minutes.

Stir the sautéed veggies into the cooked lentil-apricot mixture and simmer for 15 minutes.

Add the parsley and mint and serve warm with thick chunks of dark bread.

Cream of Anything Soup

This recipe can be used as the basis of cream soups such as asparagus, broccoli, or cauliflower.

2 cups fresh vegetables cut in pieces	Cook vegetable of choice until tender. Drain, and save cooking liquid to use later.
2 Tbsp butter **2 Tbsp flour** **1 tsp salt** **2 cups milk** **salt and pepper to taste** **fresh parsley**	Melt butter in a small saucepan over medium heat. Add flour and blend well. Slowly add 1 cup milk, stirring constantly. Cook until mixture boils and thickens. Place cooked vegetable and remaining milk in a blender at medium speed until smooth. Pour into a saucepan and stir prepared white sauce into soup mixture, blending well. Heat through and add liquid from veggies to reach desired thickness. Season with salt and pepper to taste. Garnish with fresh parsley.

Dahl

This Indian-style lentil soup can be served with rice and yogurt as a main course, since it is a meal in itself.

1½ cup green lentils, rinsed and soaked **1 cinnamon stick** **1 onion, chopped** **3 Tbsp olive oil**	Put the lentils, cinnamon stick, onion, and 1 Tbsp oil in a pot with enough water to cover. Boil and cook over medium heat until the lentils are tender.
5 cloves of garlic, crushed or finely chopped **2-inch piece of ginger root, peeled and grated** **1 Tbsp cumin seeds, ground** **1 tsp ground coriander seeds** **2 tsp chili powder** **1 can of chopped tomatoes** **½ tsp of turmeric** **salt and pepper to taste**	Heat the rest of the oil and cook the crushed garlic until slightly browned. Add the remaining spices, except turmeric, and cook a few more minutes. Stir the fried spice mixture into the lentils and add the chopped tomatoes. Heat through, add the turmeric, and simmer on low heat for 30 minutes. Season with salt and pepper to taste. **Variation:** Add vegetables of choice such as peas, zucchini, cauliflower, green beans, or spinach for something different.

Leek and Potato Soup
by Nick and Sara Craig

Another great soup to have after a cold, wet ride around Hayfield, England.

¼ cup (2 oz) butter
2 large leeks
4 medium potatoes
3⅓ cup (1½ pint) vegetable stock
1 cup (10 fl oz) milk
salt to taste
freshly ground pepper

Melt the butter in a pan and add the chopped leeks, peeled and diced potatoes and some of the milk.

Cook over a low heat for 15 minutes.
Add the stock and the rest of the milk.
Season with salt and pepper.
Liquidize the mixture and return to the heat.

2 Tbsp cream

Add cream just before serving.

Lentil and Carrot Soup
by Mrs. Gould

This is a very nourishing soup to have on a cold day. It goes best with hot, fresh garlic bread.

---

3 pieces celery, finely chopped
2 cloves garlic
4-5 medium carrots, chopped
1 cup orange (red) lentils
3 cups water or vegetable stock (recipe page 128)

Sauté the celery and garlic.

Cook the lentils, carrots, and vegetable stock for about 20 minutes, until almost tender.

Liquidize (in a blender) and add the seasonings.

Can be served with fresh parsley garnish and spoonful of sour cream or plain yogurt.

salt and pepper

Minestrone

With complete protein and lots of carbs, this classic Italian soup is a meal unto itself.

1 onion, finely chopped
2-3 cloves garlic, grated
2 Tbsp olive oil
2 carrots, sliced thin
2 celery stalks, chopped thin
½ cup broccoli, chopped
1 cup green beans, cut into 1-inch pieces
2 tomatoes, chopped
6 cups vegetable stock
1 cup peas
½ cup macaroni or other whole wheat pasta
1 can navy or pinto beans
salt and pepper to taste
parmesan cheese

Heat 1 Tbsp oil in a large frying pan and sauté onion and garlic.

Add another Tbsp oil and gently fry carrots, broccoli, green beans, and celery for a minute, stirring well.
Add tomatoes and vegetable stock and bring to a boil, then reduce heat.
Cover and simmer for 20 minutes.

Add peas and macaroni and cook until tender.
Finally, stir in beans and season with salt and pepper to taste.

Serve hot with lots of parmesan cheese, fresh ground pepper, and garlic bread.

Miso Soup

The traditional Japanese version of Miso sometimes includes seaweed. Otherwise this is all it takes to make this tasty soup.

1 Tbsp miso paste per serving
1 spring onion, finely sliced

tofu (optional)

rice noodles (optional)

Boil some water in a kettle, and place a large spoonful of miso paste per serving in a small pot.
Add a little of the boiled water to smooth out the paste, gradually adding more water until you have about 1 cup per serving.
Add spring onion and cubes of tofu if desired.
Heat through, but do not boil.
Serve as a starter or with cooked rice noodles added for a light and healthy meal.

Variations: Can also add Chinese broccoli (bok choi), and/or red cabbage, or other fresh vegetables.

"Me so hungry!"

Mom's Lentil Soup
by Nancy Smith

This is a good hearty soup and can easily be served as a main dish.

1 large onion, chopped
1 cup sliced celery
1 cup chopped carrots
3 large cloves garlic, minced
¼ cup butter or olive oil
1 large (19oz) canned tomatoes
2 cups lentils, washed
6 cups water or vegetable stock (recipe page 128)
1 tsp each: basil, oregano, and thyme
salt and pepper to taste
juice of 1 lemon
or red wine vinegar

In a large pot, cook onion, celery, carrots, and garlic in butter or oil until softened.

Add tomatoes, lentils, water, and herbs.
Bring to a boil and simmer covered for 1-2 hours, or until lentils are tender.

Season with lemon juice, vinegar, salt, and pepper.

Simmer for another 30 minutes, and add extra water if too thick.

Serve warm.

Mom's Black Bean Soup

Another one of those full-meal type soups, this is hearty and healthy.

2 cups dried black beans
2 onions
2 cinnamon sticks
2 Tbsp oil
7 cloves garlic, minced
1 tsp cumin seeds
1 Tbsp cumin powder
2 tsp chili powder
water as needed
2 tomatoes, chopped

fresh cilantro to garnish
sour cream

Soak the black beans overnight in plenty of cold water.
Rinse the beans and place in a large pot and cover with water.
Add one of the chopped onions, the cinnamon stick and bring to the boil.
Reduce heat and cook at a low boil for about an hour.
Sauté the remaining onion, garlic, and cumin seeds.
Add these spices to the soup, along with the tomatoes.
Add more water as needed, and cook until beans are tender.
Season with ground cumin, chili powder, salt and pepper to taste.

Variation: Replace water with vegetable or chicken stock.

Quickie Tomato Soup

This recipe is surprisingly similar to the famous canned variety, just as quick, and tastier.

1 (8 oz) can or jar
tomato paste
1 cup light cream
1 cup milk
salt, pepper
small amount of sugar
to taste (optional)

Heat the tomato paste in a heavy saucepan and gradually add the milk, stirring constantly, until it is well mixed.
Bring to a boil, then reduce heat and stir in the cream.
Season with salt, pepper, and sugar to taste.
Serve with hot garlic bread.

Quick Vegetable Soup
by Sian Roberts

A quick and nourishing soup.

1 medium onion
1 medium carrot
1 medium parsnip
2-3 cabbage leaves,
chopped
1 can tomato soup
mixed herbs, large pinch
splash of soy sauce
½ soup can water
5 mushrooms cut into
small pieces

Put all ingredients, except for the mushrooms, into a liquidizer (blender or food processor) in portions and blend.

Pour into a saucepan with the mushrooms and heat through.

Serve warm.

Sian's nutritional hints: "Don't get (obsessed) with your diet. Training and racing is hard enough as it is. A basically healthy diet is great, and there's nothing wrong with having the odd 'treat.'"

Sian has been racing for just seven years and is one of Britain's top racers, with numerous wins and national placings. She has also done well on the World Cup circuit, with several top-ten finishes the past two seasons. Her other interests include running, climbing, and "walking" the dog. Sian now runs (and cooks for) her own cafe in a national park in Wales.

Wales

Sian Roberts

Favorite foods: Everything vegetarian, pasta, pies, and homemade biscuits (cookies)
Pre-race evening meal: Pasta
Pre-race breakfast: Muesli, toast with beans or eggs
Race drinks: Maxim or PSP
Vitamin supplements: Vitamin C

Pro·File

Tomato Soup
by Sian Roberts

A simple and hearty dish, tomato soup is great after a long, cold ride.

---

1 lb tomatoes quartered (or 1 large 19 oz can)
2 medium onions, chopped
2 cloves garlic, chopped
2 Tbsp tomato purée (paste)
2¼ cup (1 pint) vegetable stock
½ cup (¼ pint) 1% milk
salt and pepper

Place all the ingredients, except the milk, in a saucepan and bring to a boil.

Cover and simmer for 15 minutes.

Remove from heat, add the milk, then blend everything in a liquidizer (food processor or blender).

Season with salt and pepper to taste.

Split Pea Soup

Another hearty full-meal deal soup.

1 lb dried split peas 1 onion, chopped 2 cloves garlic water as needed 2 cups vegetable stock 1 bay leaf 1 cup potatoes, diced 1 cup carrots, thinly sliced	Place split peas, onion, and bay leaf in a large soup pot and cover with cold water. Bring to a boil and cook until the water starts to get low. Add vegetable stock and the remaining ingredients. Bring to a boil, then lower heat and simmer for about 2 hours.
salt and pepper to taste	Season with salt and pepper as needed.

Veggiestock

The easiest thing to do is to buy some vegetable stock cubes! This recipe is a homemade alternative.

1 Tbsp vegetable oil 3 onions, chopped 3 sticks celery, chopped 2 carrots, chopped 2 bay leaves (optional) 1 bunch parsley, chopped 2 cloves garlic, minced 1 Tbsp pepper 5 cups boiling water 1 Tbsp soy sauce	Heat the oil in a pan and add the vegetables, herbs, and garlic. Sauté in a large, covered pan for 10 minutes, stirring occasionally. Pour on the boiling water and stir in the soy sauce. Bring to a boil and simmer for 45 minutes. Allow to cool, then skim the surface and strain into a jar or container. Store in the fridge for up to 3 days, or freeze.

Note: You can also make vegetable stock by keeping the leftover liquid after boiling vegetables.

Salads

Caprese Salad • Cabbage Salad • Carrot Nut Salad • Deb's Quick and Easy Potato Salad • Lentil and Avocado Salad • Middle Eastern Chick-pea Salad • Macaroni Salad • Mandarin Pasta Salad • Soy Bean Salad • Thai-style Salad • Three-Bean Salad • Vera's Fasta Pasta Salad

Caprese Salad
by Alex Stieda

This salad is an excellent starter to have with Italian cuisine. The fresh, soft mozzarella makes it a real treat.

5-6 fresh plum tomatoes 1 large ball of fresh mozzarella ("Buffalo")	Slice plum tomatoes into ¼-inch circles. Slice fresh mozzarella into ¼-inch circles. Arrange tomato slices on a nice serving plate and place 1 piece of mozzarella on each tomato slice.
1 bunch fresh basil	Chop fresh basil and sprinkle all over tomato and cheese.
extra virgin olive oil balsamic vinegar salt and pepper	Sprinkle olive oil and vinegar all over. Add salt and pepper and serve before pasta.

Pro·File

Bill has been racing for nine years, after a short career in motorbike racing. He is one of Canada's top mountain bike racers and also competes in cyclo-cross through the winter for a team in Switzerland. His other interests include coaching downhill skiing and fly fishing.

Chelsea, Québec

Bill Hurley

Favorite foods: Bagels with cream cheese, turkey dinner with homemade stuffing
Pre-race evening meal: Pasta with chicken
Pre-race breakfast: Oatmeal, raisins and bananas
Race drinks: Coke and water
Vitamin supplements: Quest, once-a-day multivitamin and mineral

Cabbage Salad
by Bill Hurley

Courtesy of Andy Russer, the Canadian cyclo-cross team manager. He calls it a "good natural vitamin and mineral supplement."

½ head red cabbage
½ head green cabbage
2 Tbsp olive oil
2 Tbsp wine vinegar
2 large cloves garlic, minced
½ cup raisins
1 cup peeled and chopped apples

Combine all ingredients and mix well.

Serve as a side dish with almost any main course.

(Makes enough for 4-6 people.)

Top garlic tip from Bill Hurley: "Peel garlic, and cut in half lengthwise. Remove the green stem from the middle. Removing the stem leaves the full taste of the garlic, but means the garlic doesn't stay on your breath all week."

Deb has been racing for ten years and is one of Britain's top racers, with increasing success on the World Cup scene. Along with many British victories, she finished top-ten in a number of World Cup races for a hard-earned 16th place overall in the 1995 series. She represented Great Britain in the 1996 Olympics. Deb's other interests include running, cyclo-cross, and weight training.

England

Deb Murrell

Favorite Foods: Peanut butter, bananas in porridge, pasta, Indian food, rice bake, eggplant enchiladas, rice and beans, salads

Pre-race evening meal: Pasta and vegetable sauce, salad, garlic bread or rice, naan bread, and Indian food

Pre-race breakfast: Porridge and banana, whole-meal toast and fruit spread

Race drink: Water, Cytomax/High Five Pro

Vitamin Supplements: vitamin C, occasional multi-vitamin

Deb's Quick and Easy Potato Salad
by Deb Murrell

Deb says, "The remaining dressing will keep for ages in the fridge, provided that you don't use garlic."

1 400g (16 oz) can of new potatoes
3-4 Tbsp of canned corn
2-3 Tbsp sunflower seeds
2 Tbsp chopped walnuts
1 (8 oz) can kidney beans

Dressing:
3 Tbsp olive oil
1 Tbsp wine vinegar
freshly ground black pepper
½ tsp basil
½ tsp course seed mustard
1 clove of garlic, minced (optional)
cucumber, spring onion (optional)

Wash and drain canned vegetables.
Chop potatoes in halves and quarters.

Mix together gently in a suitable serving bowl.

Place all dressing ingredients in a jar and shake well.
Pour enough over the vegetables to coat once tossed.

Serve chilled.

Deb's nutritional hints: "Never spread butter or margarine on anything. Cut the hidden fats whenever possible. Avoid chocolate biscuits (cookies). Try writing down what you've eaten (and when) for a week .. .bad diets stare you in the face!!"

Pro·File

Carrot Nut Salad

This is a nutritious and tasty salad with the ingredients providing almost all the nutrients we need.

2 cups grated carrot
2 apples, finely chopped
¼ cup walnuts, chopped
⅓ cup raisins (optional)

Combine carrots, apples, walnuts, and raisins in a large salad bowl.

Dressing:
¼ cup plain yogurt
1 Tbsp olive oil
1 Tbsp red wine vinegar
oregano, black pepper
1 tsp balsamic vinegar
(optional)

Mix the salad dressing ingredients in a jar and shake well.
Toss dressing in with salad, and season to taste with fresh herbs and black pepper.

Lentil and Avocado Salad

This makes a nice, healthy side dish.

1 cup lentils
1 semi-ripe avocado
(firm, not mushy)
2 Tbsp fresh cilantro
(coriander leaves)
1 tsp cumin powder
1 Tbsp lemon juice
salt as needed

Rinse and cook the lentils until tender (about 1 hour). Remove from heat and leave to cool.

Peel the avocado and dice into little pieces.
Toss with the cooled lentils and add seasonings.
Add salt as needed.

Garnish with fresh cilantro sprigs.

Marc is new to the mountain bike scene, having raced for just three years, after pursuing other sports interests including tennis and skiing. He has done well on the Canadian circuit and has shown promise for the World Cup circuit, but has decided instead to proceed with his medical studies. Other interests include snowboarding, windsurfing and "bedroom gymnastics." Thanks to Kate McLarty for helping with the recipes.

Marc Kazimirski

Nova Scotia

Favorite foods: Ethnic foods, curried tofu & rice (recipe included), peach pie
Pre-race evening meal: Pasta and pepper sauce — extra spicy
Pre-race breakfast: Oatmeal with fruit and fruit shake
Race drinks and food: Endura and bananas
Vitamin supplements: ginseng

Middle Eastern Chickpea Salad
by Marc Kazimirski

Salad:
1 (19 oz) can chick-peas drained (or 1 cup cooked)
4 green onions, chopped
1 small green pepper, diced
1 tomato, seeded and finely chopped
¼ cup parsley, chopped

Prepare the salad ingredients and combine them in a large bowl.

Whisk dressing ingredients together in a smaller bowl or jar until blended, and mix with the salad.

Serve in a decorative bowl surrounded by black olives and lemon slices for garnish.

Dressing:
¼ cup olive oil
juice of 1 lemon
½ tsp ground cumin
2-3 cloves garlic, minced
salt and pepper to taste

Kaz's nutritional hint: "Eat often and with gusto, making sure to lick the plate when you're done!"

Macaroni Salad

This all-time favorite goes well with many main courses and grilled foods.

2 cups macaroni
2 eggs, hard boiled
½ cup red pepper, chopped
½ onion, finely chopped
½ cup chopped celery
½ cup black olives, sliced
8-10 cherry tomatoes
artichoke hearts (optional)
⅓ cup mayonnaise
paprika, pepper

Cook macaroni noodles in boiling, salted water.
Boil eggs, rinse under cold water, peel, and slice.
Prepare red pepper, onion, celery and olives.
Drain macaroni noodles and rinse in cold water.
Place in a large serving bowl and toss with veg-etables, olives, and mayonnaise or alternative (see below).
Place egg slices and artichoke hearts on top.
Sprinkle top with paprika and black pepper.

Variations: If you are using mayonnaise keep it chilled at all times to avoid food poisoning. For a different taste, or lower fat, try these substitutes:

Dressing	**OR**	**Mayo substitute**
⅛ cup olive oil		2 Tbsp olive oil
1 Tbsp red wine		2 Tbsp lemon juice
or raspberry vinegar		1 package silken or soft tofu
fresh, chopped basil		salt and pepper to taste
½ tsp dill (optional)		

Mandarin Pasta Salad
by Mike and Emily Kloser

"Very easy and different!"

7 oz pasta wheels, ruffles, or bows
½ cup fat-free mayonnaise
¼ cup orange juice
¾ tsp curry powder
½ tsp grated orange peel
⅛ tsp pepper
1 Tbsp apple cider vinegar
1½ cups mandarin oranges
½ cup sliced green onions

Cook pasta according to directions.

In a large bowl, combine mayonnaise, orange juice, curry powder, orange peel, pepper, and vinegar.

Drain pasta, rinse with cold water and add to bowl with the remaining ingredients and toss. Add salt to taste.

Best if covered and chilled for a few hours.

Nutrition hint by Mike:
"I replace most of the oil or butter in baking recipes with applesauce. You can also cut back on the sugar this way."

Soy Bean Salad
by Christian Lemmerz

Christian sent this salad recipe to me, stating it was part of his new anti-allergy diet; therefore, it must be healthy! Serves 4-5.

---

2 cans soy-seedlings

Wash soy seedlings.

2 onions
2 apples
2 cucumbers
3-4 eggs

Chop onions, apples, and cucumbers into cubes.

Boil eggs and chop into cubes as well.

8 Tbsp sour cream
salt, pepper, chives
fruit vinegar

Mix cream with the seasonings.
Toss with the salad and serve.

Note: Low-fat plain yogurt makes a good substitute for sour cream. Fruit vinegar such as raspberry vinegar can be replaced by plain vinegar.

Thai-style Salad

Thai cuisine has a very distinct flavor, sometimes due to some obscure ingredients. This tasty salad can be made with common North American seasonings.

---

1 package tofu, crumbled
1 Tbsp oil
1 Tbsp soy sauce
2-3 cups bean sprouts

Fry tofu in hot oil until slightly browned.
Add soy sauce and fry for 1 minute more.
Stir-fry rinsed bean sprouts briefly with tofu, then place mixture in a large serving bowl.

Dressing or Sauce:
2 Tbsp peanut butter
1 Tbsp peanut (or vegetable) oil
2 Tbsp lime juice
1 clove garlic, minced
1 tsp fresh ginger, grated
1 Tbsp ketchup
1 tsp fresh chili, minced

Blend the peanut butter, oil, lime juice, garlic, ginger, ketchup and chili until well mixed.

Pour over salad and toss well.

Sprinkle with roasted peanuts and chopped cilantro. Squeeze on extra lime juice just before serving.

Tastes great hot or cold.

2 Tbsp cilantro, chopped
2 Tbsp roasted peanuts, chopped

Three-Bean Salad

This salad goes well with almost any main course, and is very tasty when served with other salads on a hot summer day.

1 can green beans
1 can yellow beans
1 can kidney beans
1 green pepper, chopped
1 onion, chopped

⅓ cup vinegar
¼ cup sugar (may reduce)
⅓ cup vegetable oil
salt and pepper

Drain and rinse beans.

Add green pepper and onion, and toss.

Mix vinegar, oil, and sugar, and adjust seasoning. Pour over beans and mix well.

Refrigerate and serve cold.

Note: If this recipe seems too strong, reduce the amount of vinegar or increase the amount of oil.

Vera's Fasta Pasta Salad
by Mrs. Vera Gillis

This tasty salad can be made in minutes.

1 package (250 g) dried pasta
(shells, spirals, etc.)
mixed vegetables
(leftovers, fresh-cooked
or frozen)
250 ml bottle zesty Italian
dressing

Homemade Italian dressing:
½ cup olive oil
2 cloves garlic, minced
½ tsp oregano
⅛ cup fresh basil, chopped
2 Tbsp balsamic vinegar
1 Tbsp prepared mustard

Cook the pasta noodles in plenty of salted water.
Add cooked mixed veggies.
Toss with Italian dressing and serve cold.

Dressing:
Pour the olive oil in a resealable jar.
Grate or crush the garlic into the olive oil.
Add herbs, vinegar, and mustard.
Shake until well mixed.
If the dressing is too tart, you can add a little sugar.

Breakfast Feeds

Apple Cinnamon Oatmeal • Awesome Buckwheat Pancakes • Banana Pancakes • Breakfast Burritos • Brake Fast Cous-Cous • Found French Toast • Homemade Granola Cereal • Oatmeal • Scottish Pancakes • Whole Wheat Pancakes with Raspberries and Almonds

Apple-Cinnamon Oatmeal

If you're like me and eat oatmeal every morning, variations are a requirement. This is my fave.

1½ cups oatmeal
1½ cups water
1½ cups milk
1 apple, finely chopped
1 tsp cinnamon
¼ cup walnut pieces

Begin cooking oatmeal with the milk and water.

Add the apple after a minute and then the cinnamon.
Add walnuts shortly before removing from heat.
Serve hot with brown sugar and milk (or cream, if you want to be like the Scots).

Notes: Cooking oatmeal with milk is a good way to get enough milk for those who don't usually like to drink it. This recipe (as with most) is even better when freshly ground cinnamon is used.

Variations: Bananas with pecan pieces, sliced peaches, blueberries, or raisins are also choice additives.

Awesome Buckwheat Pancakes
by Laurie Brandt

A tasty breakfast meal.

½ cup wheat germ
½ cup oats
½ cup whole wheat flour
¾ cup buckwheat flour
¾ cup white flour
4 tsp baking powder
1 Tbsp sugar
1 tsp salt
½ tsp cinnamon and ginger
¼ tsp mace or allspice

2½ cups milk
(non-fat or Rice Dream)
3 eggs
3 Tbsp oil

Mix all the dry ingredients together in a large bowl.

Mix all the wet ingredients together.

Add wet ingredients to the dry and mix with a spoon.

Cook on a pre-heated, oiled skillet.

Serve with yogurt, preserves, fruit, cottage cheese, or applesauce.

Banana Pancakes
by Marc Kazimirski

These hefty pancakes make a good breakfast by themselves. If eating them before an event, leave plenty of time to digest fully!

½ cup rolled oats
½ cup flour
½ cup yellow corn meal
1 Tbsp baking powder
1½ cups water
3 bananas, mashed

1 tsp vanilla (optional)
½ tsp cinnamon (optional)

Blend all dry ingredients in a bowl, then add the water and mashed bananas.
Let sit and thicken for 5-10 minutes.

Heat a small amount of oil at low-medium heat in a frying pan, and cook pancakes for 2-3 minutes on each side.
Add oil each time to prevent the pancakes from sticking to the pan.
Keep warm in 200° F oven and serve with syrup, jam, fresh fruit, and yogurt.

The appeal of eating on the course has its downfalls.

Elladee is a talented racer who got into mountain biking after riding motorcycles, about nine years ago. She is an impressive downhiller, winning the silver medal at the 1991 World Championships, and consistently placing in the top ten on the World Cup circuit. Elladee's other sports and interests include "4 x 4ing", fishing, ice hockey, and music.

Nakusp, British Columbia

Elladee Brown

Favorite foods: Brick-oven baked bagels, pancakes, cereal, fruit (in season), and vegi-lasagna
Pre-race evening meal: Rice and some veggies, pancakes
Pre-race breakfast: Pancakes or cereal
Race drinks and food: Apple juice and water, something NOT in a foil wrapper
Vitamin supplements: Garlic, vitamin C, echinacia

Pro•File

Breakfast Burritos
by Elladee Brown

These burritos make for a very hearty breakfast. Not recommended as a pre-race meal (unless you're a downhiller)!

1 tsp butter	In a skillet or frying pan, melt butter.
½ red pepper, cut into thin strips	Add pepper and sauté for 3-4 minutes. Remove pepper with slotted spoon.
8 eggs	In a medium bowl, beat eggs, milk, and salt.
½ cup low-fat milk	Return skillet to heat and add more butter.
⅛ tsp salt	When the butter foams, add egg mixture, stirring
½-10 oz package frozen spinach, chopped, cooked, and drained	constantly until done. Stir in spinach and pepper.
4 flour tortillas	Place tortillas on plates. Divide egg mixture among each and fold.
1¼ cup (8 oz) shredded cheese	Sprinkle with cheese and heat for 5-7 minutes at 350° F until cheese melts.
½ cup salsa	Add salsa and beans if desired. Serve!

Elladee's nutrition hint: "Eat, drink and be merry cuz you's gonna suffer tomorrow!"

Serve with coffee in a cactus cup.

Brake Fast Cous-Cous

Cous-cous is one of the quickest grains to cook, and makes for a really nice breakfast cereal.

1 cup cous-cous	Place cous-cous in a small saucepan and cover with cold water.
water	
2 Tbsp butter	Add the butter and bring to a boil.
2 Tbsp flaked almonds	Stir, then turn off the heat.
fresh fruit of choice	Cover, and let sit for 5 minutes.
yogurt or milk	Fluff up with a fork. If it's still a little dry, add some milk or water and cover for another minute.
brown sugar	Serve warm with chopped fresh fruit, almond slices, and yogurt or milk.
	Sweeten with brown sugar to taste.

Found French Toast (Pain Perdu Retrouver)
Jacquie Phelan

I "stole" this one by "Alice B. Toeclips" out of the *Wombats Cookbook* because it looked so good.

1 cup *either* sour milk, over-the-hill half and half or out-dated yogurt
1 egg, beaten with ½ tsp vanilla (see note)
several slices stale bread
cream cheese and jam

Mix wet ingredients together then dunk bread a slice at a time to coat all sides.
In a good Teflon pan, or a regular pan with a light coating of butter, fry until golden brown on each side. Take the pan off the heat, put some cream cheese on top of the bread slices, and cover skillet.
Make tea, then the cream cheese will be soft and you can add jam and devour (like there's no tomorrow).

Note: You can make your own pure vanilla extract by slicing a vanilla bean lengthwise into four strips, putting it into a jar with a little brandy and leaving for a month...and it will last for years! (You can usually find vanilla at your local health food or ethnic store)

Jacquie's nutrition hint: "Don't sweat the diet, but remember to shove in some fruits and vegetables — fresh ones — every day!!"

Homemade Granola Cereal

Making your own granola means you get to choose your favorite ingredients!

4 cups oatmeal
1 cup wheat germ (optional)
1 cup unsweetened coconut
1 cup sesame seeds
1 cup unsalted sunflower seeds
½ cup vegetable oil
½ cup honey or brown sugar
1 tsp vanilla
1 cup nuts of choice (walnuts, hazelnuts, almonds)
1 cup fruit of choice (raisins, dates, chopped dried figs, or apricots)

Mix ingredients together, except for nuts and raisins.

Spread out onto cookie sheets or flat pans.

Bake at 200° F for 2-3 hours.

Add nuts and raisins during last part of cooking time.

Cool and store in air-tight containers.

Can also be made without honey or sugar added, and with the amount of oil reduced.

Oatmeal
by Alex Stieda

Nutritional hints by Alex: "Always eat and drink a lot — a little at a time — especially during a race over two hours. Eat everything in moderation!"

oat bran
wheat bran
flax seed

regular cooking oats
raisins

Mix oats and raisins together and mix with 2 parts water (i.e. 1 cup oats to 2 cups water). Cook in microwave for 4 minutes on high, or in a saucepan over medium heat until thickened. Pour yogurt, fruit, or whatever you like on top and devour!
Can also add "crunchies" such as granola (see above), or Cheerios, or anything else that tastes good.

Scottish Pancakes
by Mrs. Violet

Mrs. Violet introduced these to me as a snack food. They taste great with jam when cooled. Perfect for a ride!

⅛ cup (1 oz) butter or margarine
1 egg
2 cups (8 oz) flour
1 level Tbsp baking powder
1 Tbsp corn syrup
1½ cup yogurt or milk (approximately)

Beat the egg and butter together in a bowl.
Mix the flour and baking powder together, then add to the butter/egg mixture.
Stir in the corn syrup and add enough yogurt or milk to make a fairly thick pancake batter. It should be of dropping consistency, so that you drop it from the spoon rather than pour it.
Heat a griddle to medium and brush with oil.
Drop about a tablespoon at a time to make each pancake 3 inches in diameter.
When pancake bubbles, turn it over to finish cooking.

Whole Wheat Pancakes with Raspberries and Almonds
by Penny Davidson

The best — filling and healthy — Even the name is a mouthful!

1½ cup whole wheat flour
1 Tbsp baking powder
½ tsp salt
½ cup dry powdered milk
¼ cup wheat germ (optional)
¼ cup oil
2 eggs, beaten
water, to right consistency

fresh raspberries
slivered almonds

maple syrup

Stir the dry ingredients together first, then add the wet ingredients.

Add water to create the desired consistency — thin batter makes flat pancakes, while thicker batter makes fluffy pancakes.

Pour to desired size onto a lightly oiled griddle or frying pan.
Place some raspberries and almonds onto uncooked side.
Flip when bubbles form.

When done, serve with warm maple syrup (Yum!).

Basic White Sauce • Bechamel Sauce • Bread Sauce • Garlic Oil • Good Gravy • Guacamole • Healthy Butter • Kim's Hummus • Mint and Coriander Raita • Raita Raj • Smokin' Salsa

"Where are the hamburgers?"
— *Greg Herbold*

Sauces and Dips

Basic White Sauce

This sauce is quite versatile and can be used on its own or in other recipes found elsewhere in this book.

Thin:
1 Tbsp butter
1 Tbsp flour
½ tsp salt
1 cup milk

Medium:
1½ Tbsp butter
1½ Tbsp flour
½ tsp salt
1 cup milk

Thick:
2 Tbsp butter
3 Tbsp flour
½ tsp salt
1 cup milk

Melt butter in a small saucepan, then add flour and salt to make a smooth paste.

Gradually add milk, mixing well to smooth out any lumps.

Stir while cooking over medium heat until mixture comes to a boil.

Variation: This can make a light cheese sauce for topping off various vegetables.

Prepare the thin white sauce (as above) and remove from heat. Stir in ½-1 cup of grated cheese until it melts.

Pour on top of vegetables or serve in a gravy boat.

Goes great on top of broccoli, cauliflower, brussel sprouts, asparagus, or carrots.

Bechamel Sauce

This sauce can be used on vegetables as well as for such recipes as Moussaka.

3 Tbsp butter	In a small saucepan, melt the butter and mix in the flour.
3 Tbsp flour	
⅔ cup vegetable stock	Once it is completely mixed, slowly add the vegetable stock and stir well.
(recipe page 128	
⅓ cup cream	Add the cream and spices.
⅓ cup milk	Stir over medium heat until mixture thickens.
salt and pepper to taste	

Bread Sauce
by Mrs. Violet

This is another well-kept secret recipe from the U.K. It goes well with most savory main courses.

1 large onion	Peel and cut the onion in half.
whole cloves	Place whole cloves throughout the onion.
½ pint of milk (about 1 cup)	Place in a pan with the milk and allow to simmer slowly until the onion is soft.
4 oz fine bread crumbs	
(about 2 cups)	Remove onion and add fine bread crumbs and butter.
1 Tbsp butter	
salt and pepper (optional)	Bring to a boil.

Serve warm with casseroles, meat dishes, or vegetables.

Season with a little salt and pepper.

Ginger and Tomato Chutney

This chutney enhances many Indian dishes. Really tasty!

3 Tbsp olive oil
1 tsp coriander
2 tsp cumin seeds
1-inch piece ginger root, grated
4 cloves garlic, grated
4-5 ripe tomatoes, chopped
½ cup dried apricots, roughly chopped
1 Tbsp vinegar
3 hot chilies, diced
2 Tbsp granulated sugar

Heat oil in a pan and fry the coriander and the cumin seeds.
Add ginger and garlic and fry for 15 seconds.
Stir in chopped tomatoes and season with salt and sugar.
Add the apricots, vinegar, and hot chile peppers, and simmer for 20-30 minutes.
When cool, serve or store in a sterile airtight jar.

Good Gravy

This is a vegetarian version of typical beef flavored gravy. Tasty on mashed potatoes.

1 medium onion, sliced thinly
1 Tbsp butter
1 Tbsp flour
1 cup vegetable stock, or water
salt and pepper
2 tsp soy sauce
½ tsp marmite or vegemite (optional)

Melt the butter in a small frying pan or cast iron skillet. Cook the onions until they are brown in color.
Sprinkle in the flour and add the vegetable stock or water (a little at a time), while stirring.
Bring to a boil then reduce heat.
Add the remaining seasonings as available. Salt to taste.

Note: If you add soy sauce and/or yeast extract, then no additional salt will be required.

Guacamole

This tasty dip can be eaten with tortilla chips, and/or with burritos and enchiladas.

3 large ripe avocados
3-4 Tbsp sour cream or
plain yogurt
juice of 1 lime
½ small onion, finely
chopped
cilantro to taste (optional)
salt (optional)

Peel the avocados and mash in a bowl.
Add the sour cream or yogurt by the spoonful, and stir until rich and creamy.
Add the lime juice and a small amount of chopped cilantro to taste.
Mix in the onion.
Garnish with cilantro.
Salt to taste.

Top tip from Dr. Judy Kazimirski: The avocado seed prevents the avocado from turning brown, so you can use it to your advantage in storing guacamole or half-avocados.

Variation: Use just avocado and lemon juice for a simple and tasty guacamole.

Healthier Spreadable Butter
by Laurie Brandt

Butter alone is almost 100% fat. This adds a little more substance (protein mostly), though the fat content will still be high.

1 cup safflower or corn oil
1 cup (½ lb) butter
2 Tbsp water
2 Tbsp powdered,
non-fat milk
¼ tsp lecithin
½ tsp salt (optional)

Process all ingredients in a blender (or liquidizer) until smooth.

Laurie's nutrition hints: "I'm not a big fruit eater, but I love fruit smoothies with any fruit, wheat germ, and non-fat yogurt or cottage cheese and Rice Dream (brown rice milk substitute) all in a blender. I always eat a big breakfast at least two hours before a race (which is usually in the morning), but drink a liquid meal or dense carbo drink one to two hours before a race as well."

Kim's Hummus

This is a delectable treat, courtesy of my pal Kim Hallum.

1 can chick-peas, drained
2-3 cloves garlic,
finely chopped
2 Tbsp olive oil
juice of 2 lemons (¼ cup)
½ cup light tahini
(sesame paste)
salt and pepper to taste

black olives
paprika

Mash chick-peas into a thick paste.

Mix well with seasonings, lemon, and tahini.

Add salt and pepper to taste.

Spread in a shallow dish, and garnish with olives and olive oil.

Sprinkle with paprika.

Note: It is much easier to make this in a blender, if you have one! Place chick-peas, lemon juice and olive oil in a blender on high speed until finely ground. Add remaining ingredients and proceed as above.

Mint and Coriander Raita

Raitas are yogurt-based East Indian dips that go well with curry dishes. This is my favorite.

1 bunch fresh mint leaves
1 bunch fresh cilantro
(coriander leaves)
1 cup thick-set (or Greek)
yogurt
1 tsp coriander powder
½ tsp salt

Rinse mint and coriander leaves and pat dry.
Roughly chop, then add to a blender with half of the yogurt.
Blend until the mixture is smooth and green.
In a small serving bowl, mix it with the remaining yogurt.
Add the coriander powder and season with salt.
Garnish with cilantro and keep chilled.

Raita Raj

This basic raita recipe goes well with most curries.

1 small cucumber
2 Tbsp onion, finely chopped
1 small tomato, diced
2 Tbsp cilantro, finely chopped
2 tsp ground cumin (optional)
1 cup thick, plain yogurt
salt to taste (optional)

Peel the cucumber and cut into quarters.

Remove the seeds from each piece, then chop into smaller pieces.

Prepare the vegetables and place in a small bowl.

Toss thoroughly and add the yogurt and seasoning.

Add salt to taste and chill for an hour before serving.

Smokin' Salsa

1 medium onion, finely chopped
½ cup chopped fresh cilantro
3-4 cloves garlic, crushed, grated, or finely chopped
2 cans (8 oz) peeled, stewed tomatoes, chopped (or ripe fresh tomatoes)
salt, black pepper to taste
juice of 1 lime
2 small hot chili peppers finely diced, seeds removed
1 tsp chili powder
1-2 tsp cumin powder

Mix the onion, cilantro, and garlic together with the tomatoes.
Squeeze in the lime juice and add the spices.
Blend briefly in a blender so that the ingredients mix well but are still a bit chunky.
Transfer to a dish or bottle and store in the refrigerator.
Serve in a small bowl garnished with cilantro leaves.
Makes about 2 cups.

Note: If you prefer your smokin' salsa hot, include the pepper seeds and/or use more peppers.

Baked Yams • Fake 'n Bake French Fries •
Sesame Fries with Miso Gravy •
Shredder Cheese Sandwiches (for 30 Wombats) •
Tuner Burgers • Welsh Rarebit

Quickies

Baked Yams
by Penny Davidson

Penny says, "This is really easy. It fits my lifestyle (lots of carbs and little prep time)."

**whole unpeeled yams
(not sweet potatoes!)
a little olive oil
butter (optional)**

Preheat oven to 400° F.
Clean yams well; you'll be eating the skin.
Dry off with a towel. Rub lightly with olive oil.
Prick with a knife (stab).
Place in oven on sheet of tin foil. (Yams drip so be sure to use tin foil.)
Cook for an hour to hour and a half (depending on size and thickness) and pierce with a fork to check for "doneness."
Soft means done. Remove from oven.
Eat with hands or slice lengthwise and add a little butter.

Yummy!

Note: Yams are very high in carbohydrates and go well with main dishes or can be eaten on their own for a filling lunch.

Fake 'n' Bake French Fries
by Alison Sydor

These healthy fries are baked in the oven instead of being submerged in hot, saturated fat.

potatoes
vegetable oil

salt to taste

Wash and peel potatoes.
Cut into french-fry type strips.
Spread out on a cookie sheet and brush with oil.
Bake at 425° F until they start to brown.
Toss the chips over and brush lightly with more oil.
Continue until they are crispy and browned
on all sides.

British variation:
Go to a chip shop. Order "fish, chips and mushies,"
unless of course, you don't fancy mushy peas. Remember
to order "take-away" ("to go" does not translate).
As an alternative, order a chip butty (it will probably be
your first-ever french-fry sandwich).

Sesame Fries and Miso Gravy

A one-of-a-kind snack. The recipe for miso gravy is considered top secret info at The Naam restaurant in Vancouver. (But I've just about cracked the code!)

3-4 medium sized potatoes,
washed and peeled
3 Tbsp vegetable oil
1 tsp sesame oil
2 Tbsp sesame seeds
¼ tsp turmeric
1 tsp ground cumin
½ tsp chili powder

Boil the potatoes in salted water.
Remove from heat when almost tender.
Rinse with cold water and cut into large wedges.
Heat oil in a large frying pan.
Fry potatoes, tossing with the sesame seeds, oil,
and spices. Season with a little salt and pepper.
Fry until golden brown and crispy.

Miso Gravy:
boiled water
3 Tbsp miso paste
2 Tbsp light tahini
(sesame paste)
2 tsp fresh ginger, grated
1 Tbsp vinegar

Boil water in a kettle.
Place the miso paste in a small saucepan and add
a little water at a time while stirring until smooth.
Add tahini paste and stir to smooth. Thin out
with hot water to a thick gravy consistency.
Add ginger and vinegar.
Heat until just warm.

Serve up fries and place warm gravy in a bowl or
dish for dipping. Enjoy!

What can be said about this cycling legend who has been racing off-road since it began about 15 years ago? She is awesome! She has won too many races to mention and calls sport "a religious thing." Her other interests include: teapots, quilting, writing, sex, women's lib (told you she'd been around for awhile...), herstory, travel, teaching, learning not to be afraid of driving, becoming human, meeting new friends, entertaining old ones, writing, drawing, eating, sleeping ... safe to say she enjoys life in general.

Offhand Manor, Fairfax, California

Jacquie Phelan

Fave foods: Deadly garlic spread, sourdough, Sierra Nevada Pale Ale, spaghetti alla carbonara
Pre-race evening meal: "Whatever I can forage"
Pre-race breakfast: 4 scones, cream cheese and jam, tea, "fig newtons all dried out"
Race drinks and food: emPOWERment Bars! Water
Vitamin supplements: Milk in my Brooke Bond tea

Shredder Cheese Sandwiches for 30 Wombats
by Jacquie Phelan

Jacquie says: "could be called 'feta compli' sandwiches but only after the camp is over!!"

For 30	Approximate measures for 4-5
5 lbs cheese (jack, cheddar, and feta), grated	¾ lb (4 cups) cheese
3 bunches celery, finely chopped	3 stalks celery
1 bunch cilantro, finely chopped	4 sprigs cilantro
3 bunches green onion, finely chopped	3 green onions
2 Tbsp fresh ground black pepper	1 tsp black pepper
1½ quarts mayonnaise	1 cup mayonnaise
1 cup roasted tahini (sesame paste)	3 Tbsp tahini
2 tbsp hot szechwan sesame & garlic oil	2 tsp garlic, sesame oil
olive oil if it isn't wet (greasy) enough	
Shredded carrots and cabbage to take-up	
excess oil (optional)	

Mix all ingredients together, except cilantro, in a bowl. Allot 2 slices of bread per sandwich, and spread a good portion of filling on each. Goes well on rye, whole wheat, or sourdough bread. Make half the sandwiches without cilantro and the other half with it (not everyone likes the taste of cilantro!). Cut in two and serve or pack up for later use.

151

Tuner Burgers

These are easy to make for a quick lunch on a busy day.

3 hard-boiled eggs
1 can flaked white albacore tuna
½ cup cheddar cheese, grated
2 Tbsp chopped onion
⅓ cup mayonnaise
½ apple, diced (optional)

Chop the boiled eggs and mix in with the other ingredients.
Use as filling for buttered hamburger buns or multi-grain rolls.
Bake at 350° F for 10-15 minutes, when cheese starts to melt.

You can tune a piano, but you can't tuna fish.

Welsh Rarebit

The first time I heard of this I thought it was Welsh *Rabbit!* It was a nice surprise when this toasted treat arrived. Serves 2-3.

2 eggs
1½-2 cups grated cheese (cheddar)
½ onion, finely chopped
4-6 slices bread

Chop the onions.
Beat the eggs and mix in the cheese and onion.
The mixture shouldn't be too runny — if it is, add more cheese.
In the meantime, place bread slices under a hot oven grill.
When toasted on one side, remove and turn over.
Spread the cheese mixture on the untoasted side.
Place under the grill until it starts to brown.
Remove from oven and press cheese mixture down with a fork.
Replace in the oven and grill until nicely browned.

Serve hot with "HP" or ketchup.